PUB WA[ ]
IN HAMPSI

Feb 1992.

Forty Circular Walks

The Red Lion

Around Hampshire Inns

Mike Power

"This is not the sort of book that big hikers would need. It is aimed at introducing people for the first time, to the sheer pleasure of walking"
– Paul Allen. Southern Evening Echo May 90

Other books in the series
"Pub Walks in Dorset"
"Pub Walks in Dorset 2"

Future publications planned for:
Wiltshire, Devon, and Somerset.

5,000 copies already sold
1st Edition published March 1990
2nd Edition published March 1991.

Acknowledgments
I would like to thank my wife Cicely for supporting me on many of the walks and also her help in reading the scripts, to my dogs, Sophie and Barny, who accompanied me on several occasions and often found the paths when I had failed; to the many tenants and landlords for their helpful information and Eddie Hams for his much appreciated assistance.

ISBN 0 9514502 1 2

Publisher's Note
Whilst every care has been taken to ensure the accuracy of all the information given in this book, errors can occur due to path changes, new stiles, removal of landmarks, changes in pub ownership, printing etc. Neither the printer nor the publishers can accept responsibility for any inaccuracies.

Power Publications
1 Clayford Avenue, Ferndown,
Dorset BH22 9PQ.

Printed by Pardy Printers Ltd, Ringwood, Hampshire.

Front cover: Red Lion, Chalton.

INTRODUCTION

I wrote my first book, *Pub Walks in Dorset*, hoping it would appeal to a few people but never expecting it to be a commercial success. Many other excellent publications too often leave you stranded, tired, thirsty and miles from civilisation. If nothing else the thought of a cool refreshing drink, a comfortable chair and a bite to eat is enough to push tired limbs in time for last orders.

From my correspondence it is clear I have introduced walking to a whole new sector of the population, both young and old and entire families. I hope this second book will be equally well received, both by regular and new walkers alike.

I have to admit that in the past, apart from visiting the New Forest, I have only driven through Hampshire and always thought of it as a fast and furious county with many large towns, linked by busy roads and even busier motorways. I happily admit to being wrong – Hampshire is a beautiful county of vast rolling countryside, pretty villages, lovely unspoilt pubs and endless miles of well-maintained public footpaths. The transformation from tarmac to tranquility happens almost as soon as you leave the main highways. I speak of course as an outsider, although only just; Hampshire Hogs I'm sure are fully aware of their beautiful heritage.

All the inns featured in this boooks are in rural locations. The walks, all circular and varying from 1½ miles to 6½ miles, are explained in detail with an accompanying sketch map. Some are easy, some are more challenging but most are well-marked and easy to follow. On the rare occasion when you want to walk but not visit the inn we would respectfully ask you not to use their car park; in most cases one can park close by and where possible, we have listed these areas.

It has now been proved that walking is extremely good for you, it is also safe providing a few simple rules are observed. Try to always wear suitable clothing, strong waterproof boots are best but any stout shoes will do as long as the weather is fine. If possible take an Ordnance Survey map of the area and if you are walking in misty conditions, or in the evening, a compass and a torch could prove useful. I always take a walking stick; it is ideal for clearing brambles and can help pull your walking companion up a steep slope. it can also act as probe to test the stability of the ground ahead and, probably most important of all, it can be waved to deter animals.

When walking along country lanes without pavements remember to keep to the right-hand side of the road. Close and fasten all gates. Keep dogs under control and always on a lead where there are livestock. Never pick wild flowers or dig up the plants. If we all play our part the landowners will do likewise.

Rights of way do not cease to exist just because they are obstructed or impossible to use. On the 13th August 1990 a new "Rights of Way Act" became law primarily to deal with and clarify the problem faced by walkers confronting footpaths that have been ploughed over, covered with crops or just impossible to follow. Under the new act the occupier of the land must make good the surface within 14 days of the first disturbance, or within 24 hours for subsequent operations such as hoeing or ridging up etc. It must have a minimum width of one metre for a footpath and two metres for a bridleway, and the exact line of the path must be apparent on the ground. You should report any problems you find to the relevant authority. Where the right of way crosses a field with growing crops you are entitled to follow the route even if it means treading on the crop. If the path is blocked you are entitled to remove just enough of the obstruction to get by but not to cause willful damage.

We enjoyed all these walks, we hope you will as well.

HAMPSHIRE
and
ISLE of WIGHT

Sue, Peter, Tina
June 24, 2004

The Hobler, Battramsley

It has been said that a pub is as good as its landlord – this is never more true than at the lovely 'Hobler'. It is not a smart pub but it is a great pub; the friendly landlord, Pip Steven, ensures it stays that way. The building is over 400 years old and was once a combined butcher's, baker's shop and pub. It is named after a hobler, a man who would hobble a horse by tying its front legs together so it can feed but not run off. It was on Setley Plain that such a man would look out to sea for approaching enemy ships. He would light a beacon, mount his horse and ride to Winchester to warn of the risk of invasion.

Inside the inn are two separate bar areas with wooden floors and mats. Around the walls are cases of stuffed animals, a large bookcase and various farm tools. Furnishings are simple but adequate. At the rear is a large beer garden with tables, chairs and picnic benches.

The bar is extremely well-stocked. Three real ales include Marston's Pedigree, Flower's Original and Gales H.S.B. There are a hundred different whiskeys and one of the best wine lists I have seen in a pub. It was in fact voted 'wine pub of the year' in 1986.

The inn is well-known for its good food, coming second in 1989 in a national pub food competition. The menu is regularly changed: snacks include jacket potatoes, ploughman's, pate and garlic bread. There is a good choice of main meals: 'Pork char-su' is belly of pork marinated in honey, soya sauce and sherry served with fresh veg; 'Liver Italian' is lambs liver cooked in red wine, mint, onions and tomatoes. Other dishes include chicken breast cooked in wine and herbs with an orange sauce, char-grilled venison steaks; steak and kidney pie or a tasty pork hock roasted in the oven, complete with crackling, served with an apricot sauce. A fishy special could be squid cooked with garlic, cockles and mussels. On fine sunny Sundays there is a barbeque in the garden. The excellent wine list offers 15 French reds alone, which include Château Branaire-Ducru, a fourth growth St. Julien and the prestigious first growth Château Latour 1980.

Opening hours are flexible during the week, but generally from 11 a.m. till 2.30 p.m. and from 6 p.m. in the evening.

Telephone: (0590) 23291.

The inn is on the A337 between Brockenhurst and Lymington.

Approx. distance of walk: 3 miles. O.S. Map No. 196 SZ 307/991.

The inn has its own large car park; alternatively there is a public lay-by opposite.

A short but enjoyable country walk, easy going, ideal for the whole family. It is mostly on peaceful lanes, wooded paths and forest tracks. For a longer walk you can combine this one with the Fleur-de-lys at Pilley. Both walks cross in Boldre, at the Red Lion, another pub well worth a visit.

Cross the road from the inn and go over the stile on the right-hand side of the house, following the path until you reach a stile giving you access to forestry land. Continue ahead on to the gravel drive, following it round to the left, past several dwellings, and then right over the railway bridge. The track bears left and passes several houses before meeting with a forestry lane. Turn left, go under the railway bridge and walk back to the main road. Turn right then immediately left into Rope Hill. Walk down as far as the Red Lion pub and turn left*

Continue along the lane for some distance, turning left when you reach Lower Sandy Down Lane. As you pass a couple of houses you will see a footpath sign on the left, opposite a sharp right-hand turn. Follow it down through the trees to meet the stream at the bottom, go across into the field and up to a thicket in the top left-hand corner. There you will find a stile giving you access to a field on the right. Keeping to the hedge on the left, walk up to the top corner, go over the stile following the woodland path back to the inn. One stile will bring you out into the road beside the inn, the other, via a gate, takes you into the beer garden.

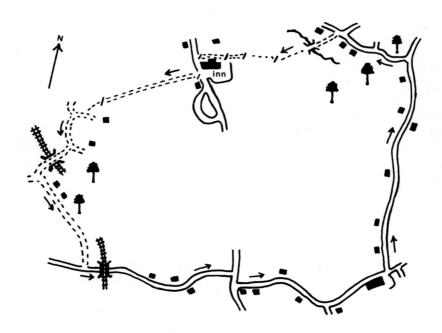

* If you intend combining this walk with the one from The Fleur-de-Lys at Pilley, continue straight ahead when you reach The Red Lion and refer to the directions on page 63.

The Montagu Arms Hotel, Beaulieu

Strictly speaking the Montagu Arms is an hotel, but is included because of its unique position at the head of the Beaulieu river, opposite Palace House, and the fact that the wine press bar is a very good place to eat and drink. Recently refurbished, the decor is relaxing with comfortable furnishings. Neat tables, chairs and benches are separated by small brass rails with hanging curtains. One side of the bar has an open fireplace, the other a food bar.

The Montagu Arms, being a freehouse, can offer a varied selection of real ales: usually Wadsworth's 6X and Marston's Pedigree with a guest beer such as Flower's Original.

Food is served in the bar both lunchtimes and evenings with separate menus for each: typically at lunchtime you can choose from open Danish sandwiches, ploughman's and salads; or for a hot meal: Somerset pork chops cooked in cider with apple and onion, pie of the day, a seafood platter, steak or a creamed fish pie. In addition there are a couple of vegetarian dishes plus some daily specials listed on the blackboard. From the evening menu, various starters include fried potato shells with a seafood filling, garlic mushrooms with bacon and homemade soup. To follow there is Jamaican chicken – chicken breast served with pineapple and rum sauce, tasty Mexican tacos and salmon baked in filo pastry. Each month, the food is based on a different theme, twelve countries being featured, from Australia in January through to Spain in December. An excellent wine list offers a choice of thirty bins.

Depending on trade and the season, the inn is open all day from 11 a.m. till 11 p.m. Sunday times are 12.30 p.m. till 3 p.m. and 7 p.m. until 10.30 p.m. Afternoon teas are served in the bar and accommodation can be arranged in the hotel throughout the year.

Telephone: (0590) 612324.

The Montagu Arms is right in the centre of Beaulieu on the B3054.

Approx. distance of walk: 4 miles. O.S. Map No. 196 SU 386/023.

Parking is no problem. Apart from the forecourt there are two more large car-parks at the back of the hotel, reached by the lane on the left. Alternatively there is a free public car park 250 yards away.

Beaulieu, despite its many visitors, has remained unspoilt. Our walk takes you down a country lane to Bucklers Hard, which was the principal naval ship-building yard during the 18th century, and then winds back through woods and along the picturesque Beaulieu river. It is easy going, ideal for the whole family.

From the Montagu Arms turn left, up the one-way street. At the main road go left, and left again on the road to Bucklers Hard, (it's about a couple of miles). Take care as you go as the road can be busy, especially during the summer. When you reach Bucklers Hard, but before entering the car park, you will see a stile on the left. Go over and walk down through the village turning left at the bottom, just pass the Master Builder's House Hotel (a good half-way stop); there is also the pretty thatched Duke's Bath Bar, a few yards further on. Continue following the path along the river bank, it is well signed, turning left at the boat-yard, and then right.

Beside a small car park you will see the footpath divides, take the right-hand path – it is very picturesque winding its way through woods, over bridges and beside the river. When you eventually meet the main path, turn right, then right again when you reach the track signed for Beaulieu. Follow it round to the left up to the house and into the field on the left. Go straight across the field keeping close to the hedge on the right, over the stile on the far side, down the short path, over another stile and into the field. Turn left, walking up to meet the gravel track then continue ahead, over one last stile until you reach the hotel.

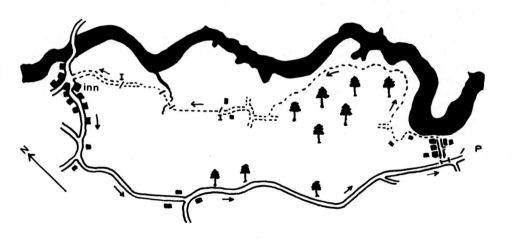

The sketch maps in this book are not necessarily to scale but have been drawn to show the maximum amount of detail.

The Three Horseshoes, Bighton

Sadly these days more and more pubs are losing their identity, some are being turned into plastic restaurants serving fast food and gassy beer, whilst others compete for stars in the gourmet food guides. I'm happy to say this is not so with this delightful village local. A pub since 1612, it is owned by Gales, Hampshire's largest independent brewery, and very well-run by the friendly licensees, Arthur and Norma Hayward. There is a small comfortable lounge, originally the inn's living area, spotlessly clean with an open log fire and an unusual thatched canopy above. On either side are built-in settles and a wall display of police memorabilia. The cosy public bar is simply furnished with tables, chairs and wooden settles. It was originally two small bars, the reason for two fireplaces today, one of which has a warm log burning stove. On the wall is a collection of old gin traps and carpenter's tools. Outside is a lawned beer garden with picnic benches.

The inn offers three well-kept real ales, Butser Bitter, light, well-flavoured and hoppy; the full-bodied H.S.B. and dark mild.

Bar snacks are available but only served at lunchtime. You can choose from an assortment of sandwiches, various salads and ploughman's. During the week and in the winter months the menu is extended to include a few hot dishes – Usually a home-made chilli or steak and kidney pie.

Children are welcome providing they are well behaved.

Weekday opening times are from 11 a.m. till 2.30 p.m. and from 6 p.m. till 11 p.m.

Telephone: (0962) 732859.

Take the turning for Gundleton off the A31 between Alresford and Alton. Continue through the village until you reach Bighton and turn right. The inn is a short distance on the left.

Approx. distance of walk: 4¼ miles. O. S. Map No. 185 SU 614/344.

Park in the inn's own car park or in the lane outside by the phone box.

An easy enjoyable walk in this remote part of east Hampshire; it is an ideal family walk, suitable for most weather conditions. Bighton is a pretty village with some lovely houses. The walk passes close to Bighton House, goes through woods, across farmland and down a long attractive bridleway.

From the inn turn left. Walk through the village, past the turning for Ropley until you reach a driveway on the left just past the farm (the footpath is signed). Go up the drive, past a delightful cottage towards Bighton House, bearing left when you reach yet another beautiful thatched property. The drive is quite short. On the right, opposite the house, you will see a path into the woods. Turn right here, and then take the left fork into a hazel copse and out into a field on the far side. Walk straight across on the grass track and then follow it beside the woods on the left, round the field until you reach a track on the left, the path is well signed. Go down bearing right, across the track and over the wooden crossing point into the field ahead of you. Turn right, keeping close to the hedge on the right, go across the far side, over the fence and stile into field ahead, over another stile until you reach a metal gate. Ignore the path to the right but turn left walking close to the wire fence, then left round the field on the far side and out through the metal gate onto the bridleway. Turn left. A short distance further on, where the track forks, keep to the left past Upper Lanham Farm. The bridleway is quite long but when you eventually reach the road junction turn left walking back down to the village. Turn left again at the road junction back to the inn.

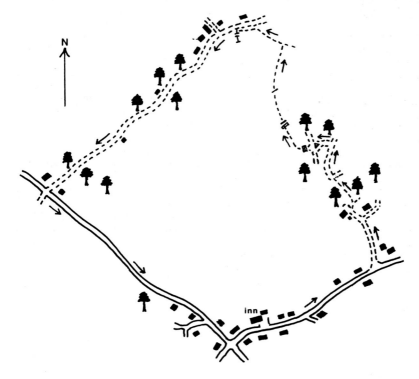

The Jolly Sailor, Bursledon

I don't think anybody would disagree that the Jolly Sailor is situated in one of the finest settings anywhere. 'The Howards Way Pub' as it is now more affectionally known is reached down a steep flight of steps; you can also come by boat if the tide is right. It sits overlooking the marina on the banks of the river Hamble. Alterations carried out in 1989 added a separate food servery and a cosy a-la-carte restaurant, the two original bars remaining unchanged; the rear bar, still with its beamed ceiling and flagstone floor, has old church pews around a large open attractive fireplace, often with a real log fire; the front bar has a collection of chairs, tables and high-backed wooden settles on the original oak floor. Two pretty bay windows give a lovely view of the yachts at anchor. All along the front of the inn and on the jetty are picnic benches.

Four real ales are served in the inn, and, although owned by Hall & Woodhouse, other brewers' beers are sold. There is Badger Best and their own light Tanglefoot, I.P.A. from Eldridge Pope and Gales H.S.B.

Food is served seven days a week from two separate menus. Lunchtime bar snacks include sandwiches, homemade soup, traditional ploughmans, various salads and whole mushrooms served in a very garlicy fresh cream, white wine and onion sauce; 'Trawl of the day' is lots of fish things and 'Smugglers pie' is homemade from steak and mushrooms. In addition, several specials are listed on the blackboard. The larger restaurant menu offers various grills including Chateaubriand. Fish features strongly with fresh salmon, fillets of lemon sole and king prawns. Vegetarian meals are available. The wine list is excellent, something to suit all tastes and pockets. Children are permitted, but only in the restaurant.

Winter opening times, Monday through to Friday are from 11 a.m. till 2.30 p.m. (3 p.m. on Saturday), and from 6 p.m. till 11 p.m. The inn is open all day in the summer from April to September, Monday to Saturday.

Telephone: (042 121) 5557.

From the A27 follow the Bursledon Station signpost, keeping left into Land's End Road.

Approx. distance of walk: 5 miles. O.S. Map No. 196 SU 490/095.

Parking is permitted in the lane outside the inn but limited to four hours stay, alternatively there is a free car park at the station, 200 yards away – you can even come by train!

An easy walk ideal for the whole family, at first through the beautiful Upper Hamble Country Park and then along country lanes and paths, and back through Old Bursledon.

From the inn go right, back up the road, over the railway bridge and bear right following the road past the railway station up to the A27. Walk straight across into Blundell Lane and continue ahead. At the boatyard keep straight ahead, go under the M27 motorway and over the stile on the right. Follow the path over a second stile and along the bank of the estuary, bearing left round the inlet. You will see a gap in the hedge, go through and over the stile on the right and along the path, turning right when you meet the wide gravel track. It winds its way through the park with short paths off down to the riverbank if you fancy a paddle.

Eventually you come out onto a large lawned picnic area with benches, a sales kiosk and toilets – an ideal spot to stop if you have brought a little refreshment with you. Continue across the lawn, past the kiosk and out into the lane turning left. It takes you through the park and out to meet the road. Turn left. The road is quite narrow and without pavements (it can be busy, so take care). Follow it round, this time over the M27, up to the crossroads. Go straight into Long Lane and immediately turn left into Bursledon Heights. Take the signed footpath on the left, at first on a tarred drive, and then to the right of the house. It brings you out into a cul-de-sac. Turn left, cross the road and go up the footpath on the right. It passes between a field and then rear gardens of private houses before emerging out into a lane. Turn left and then right into Church Lane. (The Church of St Leonards probably dates from the year 1230 and was built by the Benedictine Monks of Hamble le Rys.) Go past the church and down the footpath on the right, taking the right fork into the lane. Turn right back to the inn.

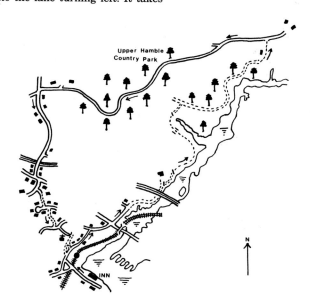

13

The Red Lion, Chalton

No book on Hampshire pubs would be complete without the delightful Red Lion, not least for the fact that it is the oldest pub in the county, dating back to 1147. It was first built to serve the stone-masons constructing the church opposite. The main bar has a low-beamed ceiling with heavy supporting timbers. Around the close-boarded walls are wooden settles with simple tables and chairs. At one end is a beautiful inglenook fireplace with its own built in seat and warm open log fire; in front is an attractive, curved wooden settle and chairs around a circular table. The other low-beamed bar, is carpeted and has candle-lit tables, also heated by a real open fire. A side extension to the bar and a rear dining room have recently been added.

At the back is a lawned and terraced beer garden with glorious views across the Downs. The inn is owned by Gales and very well run by the tenants, Ann and Brian Worth.

Three real-ales include H.S.B., Butser Brew Bitter and XXXXX – the dark sweet winter brew.

Good home-cooked food is available seven days a week. There are separate bar and restaurant menus plus daily specials chalked on the blackboards. Hot snacks can include a tasty home-made soup, steak, kidney and Guinness pie or roast topside of beef. Also available are ploughman's, salads, filled rolls and a mixed seafood plate. Depending on the season specials might include half a roast pheasant or rabbit pie. The restaurant menu is more comprehensive: to start you could choose Henry VIII Beef – tender strips of fillet beef in a delicious creamy sauce with horseradish; or perhaps Taj Mahal Chicken, smoked chicken in a creamy curry sauce with cashew nuts and salad. Main meals include a good selection of locally hung and aged steaks and noisettes of English lamb in a tangy sauce of fresh oranges and Grand Marnier. Both table and country wines are available.

Children are welcome but only in the restaurant area.

Opening times can be flexible, especially in the summer, but generally during the week from 11 a.m. till 3 p.m. and 6 p.m. till 11 p.m.

Telephone: (0705) 592246.

The small hamlet of Chalton is easily reached from the A3, about 5 miles south of Petersfield.

Approx. distance of walk: 3¾ miles. O.S. Map No. 197 SU 731/160.

The inn has its own large car park at the side and rear.

An enjoyable scenic walk across farmland and through Holt Down Forestry Plantation. Although mostly dry, underfoot parts can become muddy during bad weather.

Leave the inn and turn left, ignore the lane back to the A3, take the short stretch of lane to the right of the green. Walk straight across the Idsworth road, down the track to Old Farm, and up into the field on the right. Continue for a short distance, then go through the gap in the hedge on the left and turn right. After a while the track bears to the right; at this point head straight across the field to the metal stile in the far hedge, go over onto the track, and turn right.

After winding its way through the enclosure the track rises to meet a similar track crossing from left to right. Turn left here, up, and through the woods, then down until you reach a short gravel track on the left. Turn here. Continue ahead onto the grassy path down until you meet another path at the bottom, and turn right. Further on the track bears right, towards the Queen Elizabeth Country Park, but keep straight ahead; the short path leads you down onto the bridleway. Turn left. When you reach the road, turn left again, back to the inn.

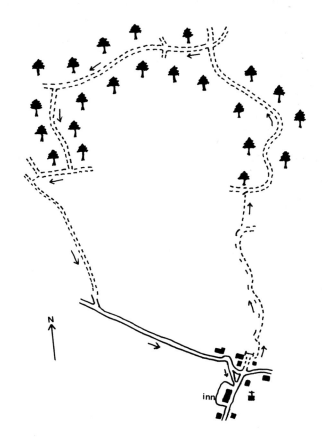

The Greyfriar Inn, Chawton

Little is known of the actual history of this friendly village local, only that it was once three separate cottages. It is a popular inn, being directly opposite Jane Austen's house – the house itself is open from April to October, daily from 11 a.m. till 4.30 p.m.; in November, December and March, Wednesdays to Sundays only; and in January and February, Saturdays and Sundays only. The inn has two inter-connected bars both with a wealth of old beams and an attractive rear beer garden. It is a Whitbread pub, very well-kept and run by the friendly licensees, Peter and Dot Lowther.

Two well-kept real ales are available: Flower's Original and Whitbread's Strong Country Bitter.

A varied bar menu offers good home-cooked food seven days a week. Snacks include sandwiches, ploughman's, various filled jacket potatoes, salads, omelettes and the French bread buster-minute steak with fried onions or garlic butter. For a main meal you can have roast beef or home-cooked ham with bubble and squeak, a fisherman's platter, steak or a home-made curry. Each day there is a special dish chalked up on the blackboard, such as home-made steak, kidney and mushroom pie. On Sundays a traditional roast dinner is served.

The inn is open during the week from 11 a.m. till 3 p.m. and 6 p.m. till 11 p.m. Telephone: (0420) 83841.

The village is well signed just off the A31, south of Alton.

Approx. distance of walk: 4¼ miles. O.S. Map No. 186 SU 709/377.

There is ample parking in two separate car-parks to the right of the inn. Alternatively you can park safely in the road outside.

Chawton, a pretty village, is probably best known for its association with Jane Austen who moved into Chawton Cottage in 1816. It was here she wrote Mansfield Park, Persuasion *and* Emma *also* Pride and Prejudice *and* Sense and Sensibility. *Our walk takes you at first through the village passing Chawton House and then on a bridleway to the small village of Upper Farringdon. The rest is mostly on farmland and, whilst easy going, can be a bit muddy in wet weather.*

Leave the inn and turn left, go past Chawton House, up the steps at the end of the cul-de-sac, out onto the A32 and turn left. Keep to the grass verge until you reach a signed footpath on the left. Once in the field bear slightly right, across to and through a pair of wooden gates, down the bridleway to Upper Farringdon. At the bottom continue ahead on the grassy track beside the play-area turning left on to the signed footpath behind the farm buildings. On the far side turn right, down the track to the lane, and turn left past the 13th-century church. Continue along the lane through the village until you eventually reach a gravel track on the left (the footpath is signed). After passing a number of bee-hives take the first track on the right. Go up to the stile, into the field and straight ahead, keeping close to the brook. On the far side go over the stile beside the gate and continue ahead crossing the brook when you reach a small bridge. Turn right. At the end of the field, go through the metal gate, turn right, cross the small bridge and turn left. Keeping close to the brook on the left make your way across to another stile and finally over one more stile into the road.

Turn left. After passing several buildings go over the stile on the left beside the brook, down and straight ahead on the concrete farm track. When you reach the field bear right, go over the bridge and into the field on the left. Keeping close to the hedge on the right, walk round and up to a metal gate, go

through and bear right across the field to a pair of stiles set in the hedge. Continue in the same direction, across two more fields and stiles, over to a metal farm gate. Walk round to the left past the house and through the gap between the small brick building and the wooden shed. A stile gives access to the field. Walk straight across to the stile opposite following the path down through the small wood to the stile at the bottom. Bear left across the field, through the removable section of the wire fence and over the stile in the wall on the far side. The narrow path takes you back to the village; the inn is on the left.

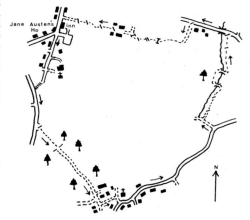

The sketch maps in this book are not necessarily to scale but have been drawn to show the maximum amount of detail.

17

The Flower Pots, Cheriton

The Flower Pots, a simple homely village inn, was built originally as a farmhouse in 1840 by the retired head gardener of nearby Ashington House. The inn has just two rooms and a lawned beer garden at the front. The cosy saloon bar has comfortable chairs, and is nicely decorated, with a small log fire. The public bar is quite plain, spotlessly clean with a selection of pub games. It is a Whitbread house, well-run in a relaxed atmosphere.

Real ale is served traditionally straight from barrels at the back of the bar. There are two to choose from: Flower's Original or Strong County Bitter.

Hot and cold snacks are available including ploughman's and sandwiches, plain or toasted.

The inn has three guest rooms – two doubles and a single.

Opening times during the week are from 11 a.m. till 2.30p.m. and in the evening from 6 p.m. till 11 p.m.

Telephone: (096 279) 318.

Cheriton, a small picturesque village on the B3046, can be reached either from the A31 in the north, or the A272 in the south. The inn is close to the village centre on the Beauworth road.

Approx. distance of walk: 2¾ miles. O.S. Map No. 185 SU 582/284.

Park in the inn's own car park or in the cul-de-sac opposite.

Cheriton is a pretty Hampshire village that frequently wins "Best Kept in County" competition. It is also the site of the 'Cheriton Fight' of 29th March, 1644, in which the King's Men, under Lord Hopston, were beaten by Sir William Waller's Parliamentarians; the battle was re-enacted in 1976 by the Sealed Knot Society. The walk is very enjoyable but not demanding, mostly on bridleways and across farmland.

Leave the inn and turn right. Go down to the T-junction, turning left towards the village centre and immediately right by the War Memorial. Walk past the garage and turn right, over the small bridge and right again into the cul-de-sac beside the school playground. On the left, beside Martyrwell House, is a footpath (the Wayfarer's Walk). Take this path up into the field and across to a stile. Go over into the field ahead and make for the stile in the far right-hand corner. It is the crossing point of the two bridleways; take the one on the left. When you reach the road, go straight across following the track along and down until it merges with another track. Keep bearing left, turning left again at the next track you reach.

You will see a small white tipped marker post on the right. Go down to the road and straight across the Titchborne road.

Go over the bridge and turn left at Cheriton mill – you will see the footpath sign. Go through the wooden gate, up past the cottage, on the grassy path to the stile. Go straight across the field, over a pair of stiles, across to another stile beside a gate, along the grass track and over the stile into the lane. Walk straight across, over the stile into the field ahead and bear right making for one last stile, giving you access to a playing field. Turn left. A narrow path leads up and through a small cul-de-sac back to the inn.

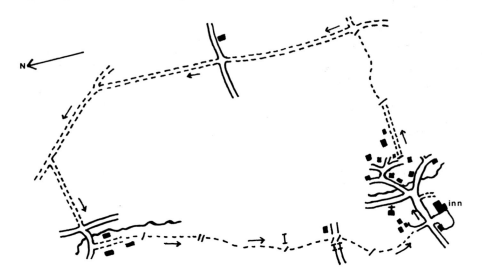

The Fox and Hounds, Crawley

Crawley is a peaceful village, yet only a few miles from the busy A34 and M3 motorway. It must surely be one of the prettiest villages in Hampshire, the centre being dominated by the village duck pond, and surrounded by picture-postcard thatched cottages. The attractive inn is about half-way up the main street. Its prominent, timbered front leans towards the road with each successive storey jutting further out. The inn is a freehouse and last changed hands as recently as July 1989. The present friendly owners, Doreen and Luis Sanz Diez, are no strangers to the trade having previously run the Old Rectory Country House hotel in Liskard, Cornwall. It is a real family-run business with their son Mark and his wife Claire doing the cooking. The inn has two attractive linked bars beautifully kept and comfortably furnished and heated by a warm log fire. There is also a separate dining room and a lawn beer garden.

There are two well-kept real ales: Wadsworth's 6X and their own 'Fox and Hound's', a best bitter specially brewed for them by Gales.

The constantly-changing menu offers an extensive, imaginative choice which includes several vegetarian dishes. To start you can have a home-made soup such as cream of cauliflower or gazpacho, hot peppered smoked mackerel fillet, hot Arbroath smokie-au-gratin, mushrooms in garlic butter, and prawn and egg Marie-Rose. The Main course menu might include seafood pancakes, stuffed courgettes with salmon and prawns, whole grilled fresh plaice or sole, home-made vegetarian crumble, and deep-fried stuffed mushrooms filled cream cheese wrapped in bacon with garlic mayonnaise. There is also a varied selection of grills. A good choice of sweets include Fox and Hounds blackcurrant and cream. Wine is available by the glass or bottle.

The inn has two letting rooms, both with en-suite facilities.

Opening times during the week are from 12 noon till 2.30 p.m. and 6.30 p.m. till 11 p.m.

Telephone: (0962) 72285.

The inn can be reached either from the A272 Winchester to Stockbridge road, or from the main A34 Winchester to Newbury road. It is on the left in the centre of the village.

Approx. distance of walk: 4 miles. O. S. Map No. 185 SU 427/348

The inn has its own car park at the rear. Parking is also possible in the road outside.

Crawley is a delightful village, remotely situated yet only minutes from the main road. The walk is mostly flat and easy going along country lanes, bridleways and forest tracks.

Leave the inn and turn right, walking back down the hill towards the village pond. At the road junction turn left (it is signed to Andover). The lane is fairly wide and straight with little traffic. Continue past a bridleway on the left until you come to a pair of metal farm gates on the left just beyond two corrugated farm buildings. Turn left here, at first walking along a concrete drive, and then ahead on a grassy gravel track passing Forestry Commission land on the right.

Eventually you meet the junction of another track (ignore the signed bridleway on the left), but continue on the path ahead into a narrow strip of woodland. The track goes on for some distance, past dense woodland on the left, before meeting a similar track on the left opposite a private drive. Turn left here. The track eventually merges with a country lane, passes several houses before reaching the village road. Turn left down the hill to the inn.

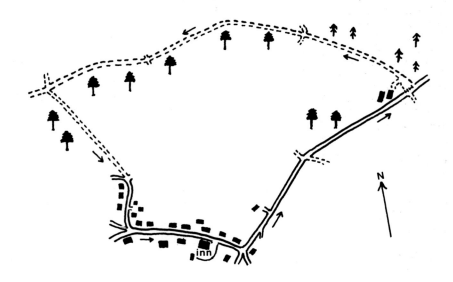

The sketch maps in this book are not necessarily to scale but have been drawn to show the maximum amount of detail.

The Queen Inn, Dummer

I would think few people outside the village of Dummer had heard of the Queen Inn until the press made the pub their own for a time when Fergie married Prince Andrew and became the Duchess of York; a subsequent party to celebrate the birth of their first baby was also well reported. Until that time the inn was a freehouse but has now been bought by Courage. It is an attractive pub dating from the 14th-century, having one main bar with several cosy seating and dining areas. The whole interior is attractively furnished and warmed by a log fire in winter.

Three real ales are available; Courage Best, Director's Bitter and John Smith's.

The inn offers an excellent menu: apart from the usual pub snacks – sandwiches, ploughman's and home-made country are soup – there are 'loaded potato skins' – baked potatoes, scooped and fried until golden and crispy, then filled with cheese and bacon and served with sour cream and a chilli dip. All steaks are fresh Scotch Angus offered with a choice of home-made sauces. Another interesting dish is a whole knuckle of ham that has been firstly simmered with vegetables and then roasted with honey, served on a bed of rice or tagliatelli. Fish dishes include fresh Scoth salmon and whole grilled plaice. There is also a selection of Continental dishes such as chilli, moussaka and deep-pan lasagne-al-torno. Several sweets include sorbets, special sundaes and Bev's home-made puddings. A small but comprehensive wine list offers four reds and three whites together with house wine and champagne.

The inn is open during the week from 11 a.m. till 2.30 p.m. and in the evening from 5.30 p.m. through till 11 p.m.

Telephone: (025 675) 367.

Walk No. 9

The small village of Dummer is easily reached from junction 7 of the M3.

Approx. distance of walk: 5¾ miles. O.S. Map No. 185 SU 588/462.

The inn has its own large car park, but limited parking is also possible in the road at the front.

An easy walk on established tracks, along country lanes and through Nutley Wood.

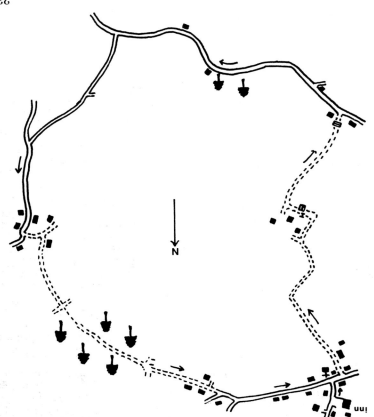

From the inn turn right, then right again at the T-junction, opposite the church (on the left is 'The Wayfarer's Walk'). Go down past the farm turning right when you eventually meet a gravel track (it is signed). Continue round and down, turning right into another track just beside a house. Go round, through the gate beside the cattle grid, down the tarred drive and turn right. Turn left when you reach the road.

After about a mile you will reach a narrow lane on the left (it's just before a bend in the road). Go up this lane turning left before you reach the B3046. After a couple of hundred yards you will reach Nutley Manor Farm. On the left, just past the main gates, is a bridleway signed to Dummer. Go up the track, through the gate, turn right past the farm buildings and up the stoney track into Nutley Wood. The path is well-defined and eventually merges with a track at the corner of three fields. Continue straight ahead down the track between the trees to the road at the bottom. Bear left and follow the road round until you again reach the church, turning right back to the inn.

The Hampshire Bowman, Dundridge

Throughout Hampshire there are a number of simple isolated country pubs, serving rural communities, that have changed little over the years. They are not smart but have a warmth and character sadly lacking in many modern-day pubs – The Hampshire Bowman is one of these. Tucked away in the small hamlet of Dundridge, in a peaceful spot overlooking open fields, it was originally a private Victorian house, built in 1812, and became an inn in 1862. It is a freehouse run by its amiable licensees, Tim Park and Peter Armstrong.

From the front porch you walk directly into the bar, originally two rooms; at one end there is a small servery and fireplace with a wood-burning stove, at the other is a lounge area with an open log fire. The inn still has its original stone floor. The furnishings consist of comfortable old chairs, wooden settles and an assortment of old tables. Around the walls are various old and interesting artifacts, pictures, stuffed birds and even the old deeds relating to the property (thankfully there are no machines of any sort). Interestingly the inn is the headquarters of the 'Portuguese Racing Sardine Club'. At the back of the inn is a large beer garden with children's play-area and a few picnic benches at the front.

Good beer is still served traditionally, straight from the barrel; the choice can vary but there is usually Gale's H.S.B. and their Butser Brew Bitter plus Archer's Village Bitter and Gibb's Wiltshire Traditional Bitter.

The inn offers a selection of bar food – snacks such as ploughman's, filled jacket potatoes and French sticks plus a few daily specials listed on the black-board. There is usually a tasty home-made soup, one main dish of the day and several sweets. In the evening there is a larger menu of both hot and cold meals; a choice from paté or perhaps a pint of prawns could precede their own hot chilli con carne; home-baked ham and eggs with chips is also popular. Vegetarian dishes include mushroom and nut fettucini and lasagne.

Opening times vary according to the time of the year. Monday to Thursday are from 11 a.m. till 2.30 p.m. and 6 p.m. till 11 p.m.; Friday and Saturdays 11 a.m. till 3.00 p.m.

Telephone: (0489) 892940.

Walk No. 10

Dundridge, a remote hamlet, can be reached either from the A32 at Droxford or the B3035 from Bishop's Waltham.

Approx. distance of walk: 5¼ miles. O.S. Map No. 185 SU 578/185.

Park beside the inn in the gravel car park.

A fairly long, but enjoyable country walk. It is mainly on bridleways and country lanes with a small section over farmland. Part of the walk is through woodland and passes through the small village of Dean.

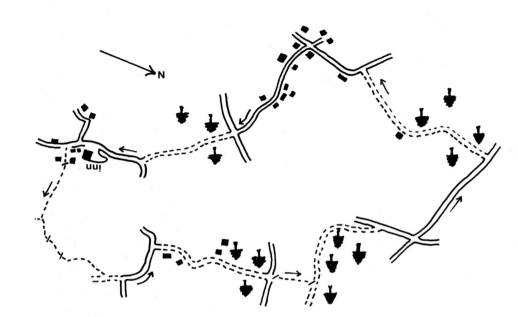

Turn left from the inn on the Upper Swan-more road, then left again at Galley Down Farm (you will see the footpath sign). Go up the drive between the house and the barn and over the stile into the field. Keeping fairly close to the hedge on the right, walk up and round, ignoring a stile at the top of the field on the right, but keep going cross-ing two more stiles until you come to a track and turn left. Turn left at the lane, walking round until you reach the turning for Hazel-holt Farm on the right. Turn here and keep to the main drive, past several buildings, through the woods down to meet the road. Walk straight across, over the stile into the field, and over towards woods on the far side. Go over the stile onto the bridleway and turn left. When you reach the road, turn right, and then left at the crossroads. Walk up the hill and down the other side for about half a mile until you reach a bridleway on the left (it is signed). The track is fairly wide and easy going, although the middle section between two fields can become a bit over-grown in summer. When you reach Franklin Farm on the left the bridleway merges with the gravel drive and bears right down to meet the lane. Turn left. When you reach the village of Dean take the first turning on the left and walk up the hill to the main road. Go straight across onto the bridleway, following it through woods and along the edge of a field, out into the lane, and turn right back to the inn.

The Farmers Home, Durley

At first sight the age of this lovely village inn can be deceptive, it is not until you are inside that it becomes apparent. It dates back to 1747, (coincidentally the same year the Whitbread brewery was founded) and prior to then it was a slaughter house. Two inter-connected bars and a cosy dining area all have attractive brick or panelled walls and beamed ceilings, supported in one room by a couple of timber props. Each room has its own fireplace, the largest with a warm log fire. The floor is carpeted with a tile and boarded area around the bar. A large collection of old artifacts, pictures, horse trappings, simple chairs, tables and wooden settles helps to create the warm and friendly atmosphere. At the back of the inn is a delightful beer garden and children's play-area with an aviary and pet rabbits. Originally the inn was owned by Strong & Co. of Romsey but became part of the Whitbread company following a take over. It is beautifully kept and run by the friendly tenants, June and Laurie Blake.

Four real ales are regularly available: Flower's Original, Pompey Royale, Fremlin's and Wethered's Bitter; and for the winter, Wethered's warm dark Winter Royal.

Excellent food is available seven days a week, all home-made using only the freshest of ingredients. You can choose from the bar menu or select one of the daily specials chalked on the blackboard. Snacks include sandwiches, salads, ploughman's and jacket potatoes; in addition there are a couple of home-made tasty soups – Farmers House vegetable and spicy mushroom. From the main menu there is a choice of grills, rib of beef, Farmers pie and home-made curry. A selection of seafood dishes include king prawns in garlic, Dover sole, seafood pasta with prawns and white wine sauce topped with cheese, even half a lobster at 24 hours' notice. Several sweets plus a small selection of French and German wines complete your meal.

Opening times during the week are from 11 a.m. till 2.30 p.m. and 6 p.m. till 11 p.m.

Telephone: (04896) 457.

A small village just north of Botley, Durley can be reached either from the B3354 or the B3035.

Approx. distance of walk: 2¾ miles. O.S. Maps Nos. 185 and 196. SU 516/160.

There is a good-sized car park to the side and rear of the pub; It is also just possible to park a few cars in the road at the front.

A short but delightful walk over farmland and on peaceful country lanes; whilst the going is easy some parts can become very muddy during bad weather.

Leave the inn and turn right. Continue through the village until you come to a stile on the left beside a farm gate (it is immediately opposite a lane). Go over down to the bottom of the field and follow the short track up to the stile, over into the field and straight across to the gate on the far side. Go through and follow the track up and then right passing the red-bricked house down to the lane and turn right. A few steps further on, go over the stile in the hedge on the left. Walk round the field, keeping close to the hedge on the right, then go over the stile beside the gate and across the field to a similar gate opposite.

Go over, and bear slightly, right across to a stile in front of a hazel copse. Follow the path through to the stile on the far side, go down to the lane and turn right. Walk round, past a couple of cottages, turning left into the drive of Durley Mill Farm. On the right is a stile (it is signed to Durley and Bishops Waltham). Go up into the field and across, keeping close to the hedge on the left, until you reach a path leading down to a stile. Go over, into the woods and follow the path to the right, through and out to a stile on the other side. Turn left in the lane and

continue walking until you reach a left turn. Follow the road round turning left when you reach the junction, then turn left back to the inn.

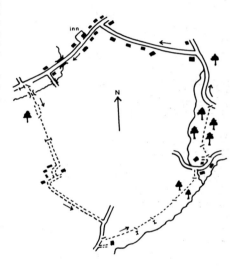

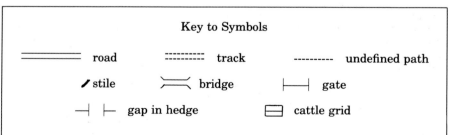

Key to Symbols

road   track   undefined path

stile   bridge   gate

gap in hedge   cattle grid

The sketch maps in this book are not necessarily to scale but have been drawn to show the maximum amount of detail.

Ye Olde George Inn, East Meon

East Meon is a peaceful village nestling in the beautiful South Downs of East Hampshire. The George, originally a farmhouse built in the 17th-century, is situated close to the church in the old part of the village. Today it is a popular inn run by its owners, Mike and Sue Young. The original living area of the farmhouse is a delightful restaurant with a wealth of old beams and two large open fireplaces. The former cattle sheds are now two inter-connected rooms served by the same central bar with, in one corner, a food servery. The inn is a freehouse.

As many customers are motorists, the beers stocked tend to be the weaker varieties. At present their is Friary Meux's Best, Ind Coope's Burton Ale and Gale's Butser bitter and H.S.B.; also usually one guest beer.

Pub food is served 7 days a week between 12.30 p.m. and 2 p.m. and 7.30 p.m. till 9.30 p.m. with a set lunch on Sundays. In the week you can choose from the bar menu or pick one of the daily specials. The food is all home-made and freshly cooked to order. There are the usual snacks of sandwiches, salads, ploughman's, jacket potatoes plus various grills. Imaginative specials include home-made pies such as steak and Beamish or chicken with white wine; There is a game casserole and stilton, asparagus, cheese, bacon and onion quiche, fish dishes and usually a hot curry. The restaurant menu is more comprehensive: from giant New Zealand mussels, rack of lamb to fresh salmon or even red snapper.

Snacks are not served on Sunday, but the landlord has no objection to walkers buying a drink and eating their own on the patio at the front. Dogs are not welcome but children are, provided they are well behaved.

Opening times in the week are from 11 a.m. till 3 p.m. and 6 p.m. till 11 p.m. Telephone: (073 087) 481.

From the A32 Fareham to Alton Road the village is signed from West Meon; Alternatively it can be reached from the A272 Winchester to Petersfield road.

Approx. distance of walk: 4 miles. O.S. Map No. 185 SU 680/222.

The inn has its own car park, but you can also park safely in most of the village roads.

A lovely scenic walk in the picturesque Meon Valley. Although a little hilly it's easy going and suitable for the whole family. It is mostly across farmland and through woods and best walked during fine weather.

Leave the inn and turn left walking down towards the church. Go through the gate and up past the church until you reach a signed footpath on the left. Follow the path to the stile at the top and go over into the field ahead of you. Keeping close to the hedge on the left continue across and over the stile on the far side, across the field to a stile set in the hedge opposite. (you will find yourself on the lawn of a private house). Walk across to the gate, out into the road and turn right. Almost immediately you will see a stile beside a gate on the left. Go into the field and turn right walking across, keeping to the grassy path beside the hedge. On the far side go over the stile beside the gate and continue ahead, down the field, to a similar stile and gate at the bottom. Walk straight across the field to the stile opposite, go over into the field ahead and across, bearing slightly right, up towards another stile set in the hedge on the far side. Continue ahead, keeping close to the hedge on the left, then go through the wooden gate, over the stile in front of you and follow the small path out into the road and turn left.

Follow the road round, crossing the stream, past a pair of stone and flint cottages and turn right into Halnaker Lane.

The lane goes up past a couple of houses and straight ahead into the woods. Where the track narrows keep to the left of the Forest gate (it is a fairly long track and although dry for most of the time can become quite muddy in places during bad weather). After you leave the woods the track continues on between fields eventually meeting the junction of another path and bridleway (it is signed). Take the footpath on the left, go over the stile and across the field towards Garston Dairy on the far side. The path then goes to the right, behind the wire fence, round over a wooden crossing point into the farm entrance. Keep straight ahead

going over the stile beside the gate, and down the concrete farm road to the road. You can see the village on the left.

If you are feeling tired or it's ten minutes to closing time you can turn left back to the pub, otherwise turn right walking up until you reach the woods. On the left you will see a track (the footpath is signed). Go up here taking the right fork through the trees until you come to a wooden gate at the top. Go through and, keeping close to the hedge on the left, walk across until you reach another gate. Go down the short track, over the stile into the field below, walking down to the bottom. You will find a gap in the hedge and a wooden footpath sign. Continue ahead up across the field, bearing left at the corner of the enclosed field. Walk straight ahead, go over the stile, across the middle of the field, over the stile on the far side, through the small car park, and down to the road. Turn right, then right again at the small crossroads back to the inn.

29

The Plough Inn, East Stratton

One of my great pleasures, apart from walking, is finding an unspoilt inn, tucked away in a peaceful village setting, that can serve me a pint of well-conditioned real ale and tasty home-cooked food – such was my delight when I visited the Plough. This unpretentious inn, once the village bakery, became a pub some forty years ago and has remained a free-house. There are two main bars – the lounge is small, cosy and comfortably furnished, the public bar is simply furnished with tables, chairs and benches around the walls; both are heated by open log fires in winter. The inn also has a separate dining room where children are welcome. At the back is a skittle-alley and across the road a large green with rustic tables and benches. The friendly hosts, Trudy, Richard and Gillian, will ensure you a pleasant visit.

For lovers of real ale you can choose from Gale's H.S.B. and Butser's Bitter or the delightful Ringwood 'Forty-niner'.

Trudy does the cooking and it's excellent, everything being home-made from the freshest of ingredients. As all meals are oven-cooked time is needed for preparation, but it's worth the wait. Each day the Plough offers a selection of specials plus separate day-time and evening menus. There are the usual pub snacks such as ploughman's, sandwiches (plain or toasted) and delicious home-made soup like beef and hare and chicken broth. The lunchtime menu includes Portuguese sardines and king prawns in garlic. Trudy's specials may include a roast, jugged hare, butterfly chops in orange and wine, braised pigeon in red wine with red currant jelly, salmon steaks served with advocado butter and herbs, or her own stuffed fillets of plaice. In the evening there is a little more choice including steak. For children there are home-made beef-burgers. For afters how could you resist baked orange sponge with an orange sauce or Trudy's French bread and butter pudding with whisky.

The inn can offer bed and breakfast – there are three large twin rooms and one large family double.

Opening times in the week are from 11 a.m. till 2.30 p.m. and 7 p.m. till 11 p.m. Telephone: (0967 89) 241.

Although being within earshot of the M3 this peaceful village is best reached from the A33, between Winchester and Basingstoke. Coming from the east of the county take the B3046, but you will need a map to find your way.

Approx. distance of walk: 6½ miles. O.S. Map No. 185 SU 543/397.

Although the inn has its own car park there is ample room in the road outside.

The Manor of East Stratton – Stratune in the Domesday Book means a settlement on or near a 'strata via' or Roman road – still has an air of old-world charm with almost every house and cottage thatched. The walk is long but fairly easy-going for most of the way; on established paths, through woods, across farmland and in part on the Wayfarer's Walk passing through the small village of Brown Candover.

Leave the inn and turn right. Go along the road for a short distance until you reach a signed footpath on the left. Turn here and follow the path until you reach the entrance to two fields. Take the little path ahead, and to the left, you will see a small post with the yellow path sign. It passes beside a wooded hollow before entering a field. At the far side go over the stile following the track ahead across the field towards woods. When you reach Thorney Down Woods, ignore the tracks left and right, but continue ahead through the woods until you reach a gravel track on the far side. Turn right walking down, only as far as woods on the left, then turn right into the field and, keeping close to the hedge on the right, go down to the bottom corner and follow the track on the right into the woods.

The track takes you through, and out, onto a gravel track. Continue ahead, ignoring the tracks to the right and left until you reach houses at the bottom. The track then merges with the lane and goes up to meet the road at Brown Candover. Turn left, go through the village centre, turning left again when you reach the church (the path is signed). Follow the track round to the church and go up the little footpath on the left, then over the stile behind the church and bear left, following the grassy tree-lined track up between fields. At one point the track meets another close to farm buildings.

Go across and continue ahead through the trees down to meet the lane beside a couple of houses. Turn left and continue ahead, across the lane junction round to the right until you reach the bridleway on the left (it is well signed). Turn left here and, keeping to the main track, go through the woods; it's quite straight-forward although it can be a bit muddy in places (on the way you will probably spot a number of wild deer). When the track leaves the woods go to the right of a small stone marker and follow the tree-lined path ahead. Eventually you reach Whiteway Farm. Go past the house and down the drive to the road, turn left and left again when you reach the church back to the inn.

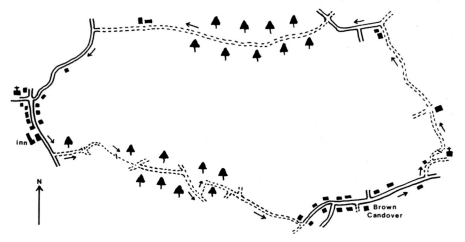

The Vine Inn, Hambledon

The historic village of Hambledon is famous, not least, for being the birth-place of cricket. The first mention of Hambledon is in a charter of King Edgar, dated 956, granting the land at Chidden. In 1750 the world-famous Hambledon Cricket Club was formed. It rapidly became the accepted authority and governing body of the game; it is therefore fitting that the village be referred to as 'The Cradle of Cricket'.

The Vine dates back to the 16th-century, its age appparent once inside. Three communicating rooms in the main bar surround a large open fireplace; one of them, suprisingly, still has a genuine old well. The attractive beamed ceilings and walls adorned with a wealth of old artefacts, plates, pictures, clocks, brass, old copper and even a boar's head, all help to create the delightful atmosphere. There is also a good public bar, heated by a stove in the fireplace, and a lawned beer garden at the back. The inn is a freehouse well-run by the owners, Brian & Eve Willis.

The well-stocked bar has a good range of drinks with no fewer than five real ales; Gale's H.S.B., and their Butser's Brew Bitter, Wadsworth's 6X, Marston's Pedigree and Morland Bitter. In addition there is Wyvern, a low alcohol beer from Gales, bottled or draught.

Good bar food is available, much of it home-made and freshly prepared. Snacks include ploughman's, filled pabs, jacket potatoes and salads. Other dishes on the menu are home-made steak and kidney pie, chilli, a choice of curries and fisherman's pie. Several daily specials chalked on the blackboards might include a fish dish, a pint of prawns, chicken kiev or macaroni cheese.

The inn is open during the week from 11.30 a.m. until 2.30 p.m. (3 p.m. at week-ends) and from 6 p.m. until 11 p.m.

Telephone: (070 132) 419.

Hambledon is situated on the B2150, between Droxford and Denmead. From the M27, come off at either exit 10 or 11 and take either the A32 or the road signed to Boarhunt – the village is well signed. The inn is on the left in the main village road.

Approx. distance of walk: 4½ miles. O.S. Map No. 196 SU 645/150.

Parking at the inn is very limited but you should find no problem outside in West Street.

A lovely walk, fairly easy going, with just the occasional muddy patch. At first through the village and on the part of the Wayfarer's Walk; then along bridleways and paths, through woodland and over farmland.

From the inn turn left, walk through the village turning left opposite the post office into High Street. Go up to the church, through the gate, and left round the churchyard until you reach a marked footpath on the left. Take this path down to the metal gate, go through and across the field, out through the gate on the far side into a cul-de-sac. Continue straight ahead across a grassy area beside some chalets down to meet the road. Turn right, cross the road and go up the grassy signed footpath on the left.

The path is fairly steep winding its way through woods to a stile at the top. Go over and take the wide track ahead until it bears left by a field. At this point follow the narrow track on the right (you will see the W.W. path markers on the trees). It takes you to a stile giving access to a large field. Go across the field, through a line of trees, and over a stile on the far left-hand side into the next field. Bearing slightly to the right, go across to meet the lane on the far side.

Walk across, go over the stile and follow the track, across the field to the far side. Bear left, through the gap, into the field ahead. Looking for the path markers, follow the track beside the hedge across the stile next to the gate on the far side. Leaving the Wayfarer's Way, go over the stile and turn left on to the bridleway, down the road (it can often be a bit muddy). When you reach the road turn right, go down and round until

A lovely brick and timbered barn on raised saddle stones to be seen during the walk

33

you come to a couple of cottages; immediately opposite you will see a path on the left — take this path (it is fairly long and goes down to meet a quiet country lane). Turn left walking up to the T-junction and go straight across, through the gap into the field (the footpath is signed).

Walk across, bearing left as you go, in the direction of a farm-house. When you reach the drive-way turn left through the farm, go over the gate and follow the track across the field alongside the fence until you reach a stile. Go over into the field ahead and up, bearing right and to the left of a house, out into the road at the top. Turn right, walk round and down until you reach a signed footpath on the left. It is a grassy path passing the back wall of a garden. When you reach a stile go into the field, across to a second stile, and over on to the footpath. It is a narrow track meeting a similar one a few yards further on. Take the right fork back down to the main road; go straight across into West Street back to the inn.

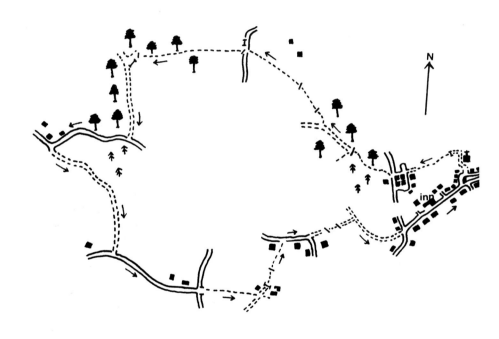

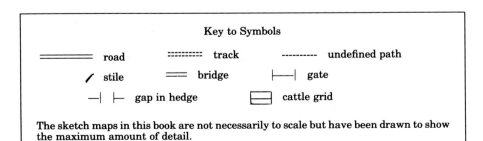

Key to Symbols

road   track   undefined path

/ stile   bridge   gate

gap in hedge   cattle grid

The sketch maps in this book are not necessarily to scale but have been drawn to show the maximum amount of detail.

Bucklers Hard, walk No. 2

Jane Austen's House, Chawton, walk No. 6

The Prince of Wales, Hammer Vale

High up in a sunny position overlooking the pretty Hammer Vale sits the Prince of Wales inn, and, although built as recently as 1926, it has a good atmosphere. One end has tables and chairs for those wishing to eat; the other is more sociable with just a couple of tables but plenty of standing room on the close-boarded floor and a warm wood-burning stove. It is the most easterly inn in the book actually bordering three counties, Hampshire, Surrey and West Sussex and is owned by Gales, Hampshire's largest independent brewery.

Good real ale is still served traditionally, straight from the barrel. You can choose from H.S.B., Butser's Brew Bitter and, from autumn onwards, XXXXX their winter warmer.

Good food is available seven days a week: you can choose something from their large set menu or one of the daily specials, such as swiss mushrooms on toast, ploughman's, sandwiches toasted to order, filled jacket potatoes, burgers; and also as a snack, or just a starter, there is soup of the day, whitebait and breaded garlic mushrooms. Main meals include various grills, omelettes and fried fish. Other seafood available are mussels in garlic butter, grilled king prawns and fresh grilled sardines, all served with granary or garlic bread. The evening menu is more extensive. It includes spare ribs in barbecue sauce, 'Hammer Trout', swordfish cutlet with cheese and parsley and chicken breast filled with prawn and lobster, to name but a few. Vegetarian meals are usually available. A selection of sweets include home-made apple pie and treacly roly poly pudding. A good wine list offers a selection from France, Germany, Italy and Yugoslavia. A roast lunch is served on Sunday.

The inn is open during the week from 11 a.m. till 3 p.m. and 6 p.m. till 11 p.m. Telephone: (0428) 52600.

From Liphook go north on the A3 and take the turning on the right signed to Hewshott; follow the lane until you reach the inn.

Approx. distance of walk: 2½ miles. O.S. Map No. 186 SU 868/327.

The inn has its own fair-sized car park.

The Hammer Vale is a lovely walking area with miles of public footpaths. We decided to make this a short walk suitable for the whole family. The going is easy, but not recommended during wet weather, when it can become quite muddy. The first part of the walk is on country lanes; the second along bridleways. There is a beautiful walking area on the other side of the A3 around the lakes at Waggoners Wells owned by the National Trust.

Start at the back of the inn and go up the footpath by the picnic beaches following the path round to the left and down to meet the lane. Turn right. Keep to the lane for some distance until you eventually reach Hewshott House. On the left, before the house, is a signed bridleway. Go down to the bottom, over the river and under the railway bridge to meet another bridleway and turn left.

Continue ahead, close to the railway line, ignoring the paths off to the right. When you reach a small gate go through into the field and across to a stile on the far side. It brings you onto the bridleway again. Keep straight ahead until you reach the lane and turn left; walk around, over the bridge and up the lane on the left back to the inn.

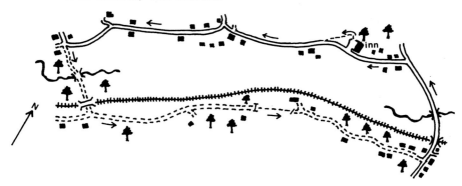

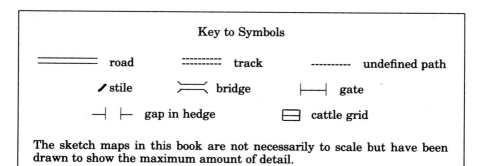

Key to Symbols

═══════ road ⁻⁻⁻⁻⁻ track ⁻⁻⁻⁻ undefined path

✒ stile ⤵ bridge ⊢─┤ gate

─┤ ├─ gap in hedge ⊟ cattle grid

The sketch maps in this book are not necessarily to scale but have been drawn to show the maximum amount of detail.

The Old Beams Inn, Ibsley

The atmosphere in this lovely, thatched 14th-century roadside inn is very much that of a busy restaurant, attracting diners from all around the area. Greeted by a warm coal fire in the entrance, you can either go into the cosy old-world beamed restaurant or through to the large bar at the back. Divided by a central screen and log effect fire, the bar has been well built and decorated, harmonising well with the original pub. Down one side is an efficient food servery, the cold food displayed in large cabinets; at the back doors lead through to a large summer terrace.

The Old Beams is a freehouse, able to offer a varied selection of well-kept real ales. There are two from the local Ringwood brewery, their Best Bitter and the delightful Old Thumper. Others regularly available are Wadsworth's 6X, Burton Ale, Bishop's Tipple and the Strong Royal Oak from Eldridge Pope.

Food is served lunchtime and in the evening in both the bar and the restaurant. The menu, chalked on blackboards at the food servery, offers a good choice of snacks from sandwiches, ploughman's and serve-yourself salads, to home-made soup and steak and kidney pie. There is usually a curry and a daily roast. Other dishes might include rabbit pie, pheasant in red wine or osso buco, plus several fish dishes: whole plaice, sole, halibut and salmon. The a-la-carte restaurant offers a large selection of very good imaginative meals: 'Blinze' is a savoury pancake of prawns and crabmeat coated in cream and glazed. Turtle soup is served laced with sherry. A wide selection of main meals includes venison casserole and 'tournados Henry VIII' – fillet steak with stilton cheese in a whisky and onion sauce.

Children are allowed in the eating areas. The inn is open during the week from 10.30 a.m. till 3 p.m. and from 6 p.m. until 11 p.m. (10.30 p.m. in the winter).

Telephone: (0425) 473387.

The inn is on the A338 at Ibsley, between Fordingbridge and Ringwood.

Approx. distance of walk: 6 miles. O.S. Map No. 195 SU 150/095.

There is ample room to park in front of the inn or in the service lane outside the church.

A fairly long, but most enjoyable walk across New Forest heathland, through the small villages of Mockbeggar and South Gorley, down peaceful forestry roads and across farmland. It is fairly dry and easy going, best walked on a dry day.

Leave the inn and turn left, go past the church and take the turning left to Mockbeggar. When you reach the village go over the crossroads and up the lane ahead by the church. Continue walking on to the gravel track, past several houses and through a half-wooden gate up onto Ibsley Common. Keep to the main track (it is well-defined), past the triangulation point on the left and on until you reach a track on the left. It passes a couple of war-time bunkers before reaching the crest of a hill. Walk down and bear left at the bottom taking the track up the hill. At the top, after a short distance, you will see a path going off to the right. Take this path, you will see houses on the distant horizon. It starts level and then descends steeply down Dorridge Hill. At the bottom ahead of you, is a gravel track. Go past the houses, down the road and turn left (it is signed to South Gorley).

After about a mile-and-a-half (when you reach the village), turn left on the road to Ringwood. Go past several cottages turning right when you reach Ibsley Drove (it is a gravel track and there is a gate beside a cattle grid). Walk down for short distance

until you reach the entrance to Merrilea Farm on the left. Go over the stile at the right of the drive into a small field, across to another stile, then straight across the field to another stile on the far side. Go across the track; ahead of you is a series of well-maintained stiles which bring you out onto a track by a stable block. Climb over the wooden fence to the left of the stables, and walk across the field to the hedge on the left. Just to the right of a small oak tree is a stile; go over and bear right meeting the hedge on the right. Keeping close, walk along until you reach a stile on the right, go into the adjoining scrubland, turn left, and walk close to the hedge on the left until you reach a wooden crossing point giving access to a large field. Still keeping close to the hedge walk across over to two stiles on the far side. Go over the one on the right and bear right, across the field, keeping close to the hedge on the right. Go through the two metal gates, down the driveway of the house, and out onto the road. Turn left back to the inn (take care as the pavement is quite narrow and the road extremely busy).

The High Corner Inn, Linwood

The High Corner has been for a number of years the ideal family pub. Tucked well away deep in the New Forest, it is an attractive inn draped with wisteria in summer and heated by an open fire in the winter. The main building was built in the 1700s as a farm; now the old stables have been connected to the main inn with a linking building. The Stable Room is used for conferences and doubles as a very pleasant family room; the main bar is very cosy with beamed walls and ceilings with several rooms leading off. Outside is a large garden with picnic benches and a barbecue area. If you feel energetic after your walk, the inn even has its own squash court. The High Corner is a freehouse, well run by the owners, Lin & Roger Kernan.

A well-stocked bar includes draught Murphey's stout, Flower's Original, Marston's Pedigree and Wadsworth's 6X.

The inn is very popular for its food: from the set menu there is a choice of starters including soup; main meals include home-made steak and kidney pie with mushrooms, chicken Maryland, gammon, fresh Avon trout, various omelettes and a mixed grill. There are, of course, the usual snacks such as ploughman's and sandwiches plus others, like sausage platter and 'old smokey' – a fish pie with smoked haddock, tomato and cheese sauce, served with crusty bread. There are several tempting sweets to follow plus an excellent wine list with a selection from France, Italy, South Africa, Bulgaria and Chile. The inn also offers an all-day Sunday carvery, a three course meal served from 12 noon.

Opening times are fairly flexible depending upon the time of year but normally open all day during the summer from 11 a.m. till 11 p.m. and in the winter from 11 a.m. till 2.30 p.m. and in the evening from 7 p.m. until 10.30 p.m. The inn is able to offer accommodation – six new bedrooms have just been added and furnished to a very high standard.

Telephone: (0425) 473973.

Linwood is signposted from the A338, Ringwood to Fordingbridge road. Continue through the woods onto the heath. The pub is signposted left, down a long gravel drive.

Approx. distance of walk: 3¼ miles. O.S. Map No. 195 SU 197/107.

The inn has ample parking which includes a couple of overspill car parks. Parking is not permitted in the gravel drive.

A most enjoyable New Forest walk ideal for the whole family, through woods and across heathland. The going is easy, mostly on wide gravel tracks, although during wet weather it can be very muddy in places.

Leave the inn, go out on to the gravel drive and turn left. Walk down towards Dockens Water and take the left fork. Immediately go right over the wooden bridge and follow the gravel track up to the forest gate, go through and bear right, up the grassy path onto the heath. As you near the top take the path off to the right between some lone pine trees and the wire fence of the enclosure. Continue round, turning right when you reach the wooden gate into Hasley Enclosure. Go up the short track onto the main drive, and turn right (it is a mixed wood with a predominance of chestnut trees). When you reach the far side, go out through the wooden gate and continue ahead of the track, turning right when you come to a sandy path. Follow it down to the stream at the bottom, go over the bridge and into the woods ahead. Keeping close to the wire fence on the right, walk up to and over the gravel drive, past the gate up until you reach a second gate (numbered 89). Go through, and follow the gravel track through the woods for some distance until you reach a path off to the left leading to a wooden gate. Go through, across the forest lawn, over the wooden bridge and turn left. Follow the grassy path up and through the trees. It is not very well-defined but easy to follow. At the top, bear right, walking down to meet the gravel drive and turn right, back to the inn.

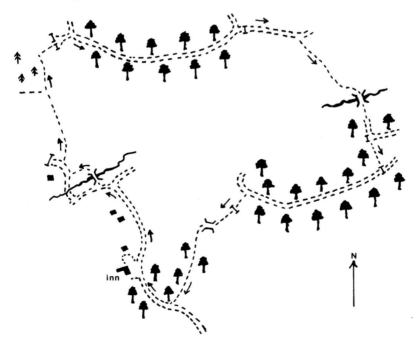

The Trusty Servant, Minstead

Within the New Forest are many small villages, miles of beautiful walks and many lovely local pubs. Minstead is typical – situated close to the end of the M27 it is popular with summer visitors, many of whom are Sherlock Holmes fans paying homage to his creator, Conan Doyle, who is buried with his wife on the furthest south side of the churchyard. The church itself is very interesting; it dates back to the 12th-century and is one of only two listed in the Domesday Book. Interestingly it has private boxes as well as pews (one of them even has its own fire-place).

The Trusty Servant is a simple village pub, rebuilt in 1901 and owned by Whitbreads. There are two rooms: a small public bar with a wood-burning stove and a cosy lounge, simply, but comfortably furnished. It is a warm and friendly local made more so by the amiable tenants, Dave and Lydia Mills. From the moment you walk through the door you are made to feel welcome.

Two well-kept real ales are delivered by hand pump: Flower's Original and Strong Country Bitter. In the summer you can enjoy your drink sat around the tree on the village green in front of the inn.

A small menu offers a choice of very good, freshly-prepared snacks with several hot daily specials listed on the blackboard – there are sandwiches (plain and toasted, with a variety of fillings), forester's platter with gammon and cheese, various ploughman's and a warming bowl of home-made soup; cold home-cooked gammon is served with chips. Other specials include lasagne and cottage pie, with home-made sweets such as apple pie and blackberry crumble to complete your meal.

Children are not allowed in either bar but dogs are welcome. The inn has three letting rooms and can offer bed and breakfast.

Opening times, Monday to Friday are from 11 a.m. till 2.30 p.m. and 6 p.m. till 11 p.m. Saturday 11 a.m. till 4 p.m. and 7 p.m. till 11 p.m.

Telephone: (0703) 812137.

The village of Minstead is just over a mile from the A31 at the end of the M27 (it can only be reached from the west-bound carriageway). Alternatively you can turn off the A35 at Lyndhurst.

Approx. distance of walk: 2½ miles. O.S. Map No. 195 SU 282/110.

Park beside the inn or by the village green.

A lovely walk, one of my favourites, through this historic New Forest village. It is easy going, along country lanes and woodland paths, ideal for the whole family.

Leave the inn and turn right up the lane to the church (well worth a visit). On the right is a signed footpath; go through the gates and follow it round the field, through another gate and into a small wood. Follow the path to the bottom, go through the gate and turn right up to the road. Walk across and go up the lane beside the brook towards Furzey Gardens. At the end of the lane bear left, and then left again when you reach the gravel drive, just past Furzey cottage (the gallery and cottage is open to the public 10 a.m. to 5 p.m. approx.).

Go across the carpark and down the path into the woods (it is signed). Take the right fork down to the bottom, go over the bridge and stile, up the bank, and over the stile at the top into the field on the left. Walk down to the right-hand corner, go over the stile and follow the path up to meet the lane. Go straight across up and round the lane opposite to the T-junction, and turn left. Walk down to meet the main village road and turn right, back to the inn.

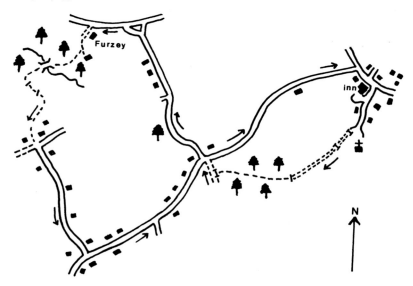

Minstead Church

A New Forest Pony

The Isle of Wight

Old Town Hall, Newtown

We decided to include the Isle of Wight within the Hampshire book, not because it lacks good pubs, nor because of a lack of good walks (in fact the island probably has more pubs per square mile than anywhere else in the U.K. and absolutely miles of well-maintained public footpaths), but because a lot of pubs are very commercial as the island depends on tourism for its economy. There are all types of pubs from the small local to the larger-style ones specialising in entertainment with family rooms, children's menus and play area.

We looked for individual pubs, remotely situated, offering both good food and real ale with an interesting circular walk. On that basis it would have been difficult to have found forty. Three of the inns are owned, inevitably by Whitbreads, as they own more than one hundred on the island, but we are pleased to be able to include one owned by Burts, the only local independent brewery.

The walks (nos. 19 to 22) vary in length from 1½ to 4¾ miles. Two of them take you high up on to the downs; one is a short coastal walk; the other, in part, follows the bank of a brook. We enjoyed them, hopefully you will as well.

The Hare and Hounds, Downend

Adjacent to Robin Hill, high up on the Downs above the Arreton Valley, is the lovely old, thatched Hare and Hounds. The main bar of this unpretentious inn has a beamed ceiling, flag-stoned bar area and a large inglenook fireplace with a warm log fire in winter. It is simply furnished with tables, chairs and wooden wall settles; there is a small lounge to the side of the main bar, a family room up a short flight of steps, and at the back of the inn is a separate attractive restaurant. A fair bit of history is attached to the inn – the beam above the inglenook fireplace once formed part of the gibbet which stood on Gallows Hill (adjacent to the inn), last used at the execution of Michael Morey who was hanged for the murder of his grandson in 1753. The hangman kept a tally of his victims by cutting a notch in the beam every time it was used – The notches together with the date, 1735 can still be seen. In a small glass case above the fire is a macabre human skull, said to be that of Michael Morey himself.

The inn is owned by Burt & Co., the Island's only independent brewery. Two real ales are available: B.M.A., a pleasant dark mild and 'Veeps', as it is known locally, a malty best bitter.

The tenants, Martin and Dollie Crockford, offer an interesting range of both hot and cold food: there are the usual snacks such as ploughman's, jacket potatoes, various pies and salads. Starters include soup, pate, prawns in garlic or mushrooms in a cream sauce, and for main course, there is usually a tasty home-made curry, various steaks, honey roast ham or, if you prefer fish, rainbow trout stuffed with prawns and almonds. Daily specials chalked on the blackboard in the bar might include a home-made cottage pie cooked in draught Guinness, served with saute potatoes or, for vegetarians, macaroni with mixed vegetables.

The inn is open during the week from 11 a.m. till 3 p.m. and in the evening from 7 p.m. till 11 p.m. During the busier summer season the hours are extended to all-day opening.

Telephone: (0983) 528159.

Adjacent to Robin Hill, this lovely old inn can be reached from either the A3054 or the A3056.

Approx. distance of walk: 4½ miles. O.S. Map No. 196 SZ 533/876.

There is ample parking space on either side of the inn.

An enjoyable walk through the woods, over downs, on bridleways and farmland. It is mostly easy going, although a little hilly and can be muddy during bad weather. It takes in Arreton Manor, a superb example of an English manor spanning the Elizabethan and Jacobean periods, the history of which goes back to before Alfred the Great, who mentions Arreton in his will of A.D. 885.

From the front of the inn turn left heading eastwards on the Brading road (it can be busy so take care). A couple of hundred yards further on you will come to a gravel track on the left, turn here and walk down towards the farm. At one point going through a small metal gate beside a cattle grid, across a field, through a similar gate beside another grid and up to the entrance of Combley Farm. Go through the gate, across the yard, through the gate opposite and take the track on the left. After only a short distance, and before reaching the chalets at the top of the track, go into the field on the left. Walk round the field, keeping close to the hedge on the left. At the top far corner is a small gate, go through and up the narrow path adorned on either side with an abundance of ferns and primroses, turning left when you reach the drive at the top. At the road turn left, going past the W.W.C. tip, turning right onto public footpath no. 92. Go over the stile beside the gate, across to a second stile and into the field ahead. Bearing left, walk up and across the field to a stile set in the far hedge. Walk across the road, through the gate opposite onto public footpath no. A25a. The track runs beside the hedge, round to the right and across to a gate. Go out onto the bridleway and turn left.

When you reach the lane at the bottom go straight across the road and over the stile. Bear right across the field to a stile set in the hedge, just behind the electricity pole. The path descends down through a wood to meet a bridleway at the bottom. Turn left. Continue along the bridleway, past a couple of houses, left past Great East Standen Manor Farm until you reach the top of the hill.

Another bridleway crosses from the left to right; there is also a stile on the left. You can take either; we prefer the bridleway, although it can sometimes be muddier. Turn left here and walk down until you reach the road. Turn right, and then left on to the Shanklin road. Go down only as far as the White Lion, another lovely old pub worth a visit, and turn left.

If you want to visit Arreton Manor the House is open from one week before Easter until the end of October, Monday to Fridays inclusive. 10 a.m. to 6 p.m., Sundays 2 p.m. to 6 p.m. It is closed on Saturdays). Go up to and left round the church onto public footpath no. A12. Keep to the side of the field at the top, go up the steps, over the stile and bear left across the downs making for a stile in the far left top corner. Go out into the road and turn right back to the inn.

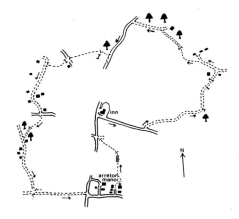

The Buddle Inn, Niton

Sitting high above St. Catherine's Lighthouse, in the southern most tip of the Island, is the attractive Buddle Inn. There have been numerous suggestions about the origin of the unusual name – the most generally accepted being the old English word 'bothele', meaning the dwelling place. The exact age of the inn is unknown, but there is said to have been a three-bedroomed cottage on the site around the year 1500; the present building was a farm and only granted its first licence in 1850. The exterior remains much the same but recent alterations inside have added a separate food servery and dining area. The original flagstone floor still exists together with an enormous old inglenook fireplace and some fairly old tables and chairs. Outside there are picnic benches on the lawn and a barn on the side of the inn has been converted into a children's play area.

The inn is a Whitbread House very well-run by the friendly licensees, Pat and John Bourne.

A selection of real ales include Pompey Royal, Strong Country Bitter, Flower's Original, Marston's Pedigree, Wethereds S.P.A. and Fremlin's Bitter plus, usually, a guest beer.

Good food is served daily: you can choose something from the set menu or pick one of the daily specials chalked on the blackboard. Simple snacks include tasty home-made soup, prawns on the shell or a ploughman's; there are various flans, a chilli and the inn's own home-cooked gammon and from the griddle there is a choice of steaks. To accompany your meal there is wine by the glass, bottle or carafe.

During the summer months, from Easter to mid-September, and during the half-term holidays, the inn is open in the week from 11 a.m. till 11 p.m. The rest of the year from 10 a.m. till 3 p.m. and in the evening from 6 p.m. till 11 p.m..

Telephone: (0983) 730243.

From the A3055 take the turning to St. Catherine's Point.

Approx. distance of walk: 1½ miles. O.S. Map No. 196 SZ 504/758.

The inn has its own large car park opposite.

A short, but interesting walk, down to Knowle's Farm and St. Catherine's Lighthouse. Certain parts are quite steep and a bit tricky. It is bracing walk in all but the calmest of weather conditions.

From the inn turn right along the village road and continue ahead onto the drive down to the National Trust's Knowle's Farm. Just before reaching the entrance gate, go over the wooden gate on the left and across to the corner of the lighthouse. Go left over the stile and immediately left over the wall of the lighthouse. Follow the path to the far side and then, out through the gap, down the wooden steps to the cliff top. The path goes up to a gate, across open fields to a gate on the far side and through into a small caravan park. Keep to the left and go up the gravel track. As you round the bend you will see a signed footpath on the left; take this path up the steps which will bring you out opposite the inn.

49

The New Inn, Shalfleet

Real pubs are getting harder to find these days but you do not have to look far to find this gem. Only four miles from the ferry at Yarmouth, the New Inn is on the Newport road in the pretty village centre of Shalfleet. It is a popular inn, and deservedly so, drawing people from all over the Island to sample the lovely atmosphere and excellent seafood. Built in 1746, on the site of the old church-house, it remains uncommercialised and unhurried despite its popularity. The inn has two attractive bars with a lawned beer garden at the back. The public bar has a lovely original flagstone floor, scrubbed deal tables with wooden wall settles beside a large open stone fireplace with a warming log fire in the winter; the other bar is more comfortably furnished with neat tables and chairs on a carpeted floor.

Real ale is still served traditionally, straight from casks at the back of the bar: you can choose from Flower's Original, Pompey Royal and Strong Country Bitter; two other beers; Gale's H.S.B. and Marston's Pedigree are available at certain times.

Chris Vanson only took over this Whitbread Inn in 1989 but is still happily maintaining its reputation for good food. Whilst snacks such as ploughman's and sandwiches are always available, the emphasis is on seafood; mussels are the speciality – you can have them coooked in wine or with garlic. A blackboard in the bar lists all the daily specials: there is an excellent choice of locally-caught fresh fish such as cod, salmon, plaice, Dover sole and even St. Catherine's shark; shellfish is much in evidence with local crab and lobster dishes. Beside fish there is home-cooked Virginia ham, lasagne, poacher's pie, steak and the famous New Inn 'Blow Your Mind' chilli. Children are welcome and well catered for with their own menu. A choice of wines are available from a large list.

Weekday opening times throughout the year are from 11 a.m. till 3 p.m. and 6 p.m. until 11 p.m. Summer time hours are more flexible with all-day opening on Saturday.

Telephone: (098 378) 314.

The inn is in the centre of Shalfleet on the main A3054 between Yarmouth and Newport.

Approx. distance of walk: 3¼ miles. O.S. Map No. 196 SZ 415/893.

The inn has its own small car park at the rear and there is also a public car park a few yards further down the lane.

Shalfleet is a delightful village just a stroll from the old quay and the Newtown nature reserve. Originally the island's capital, Newtown is today no more than a quiet river inlet; only the splendid town hall, built in the 17th century, is a lone reminder of this once-important area. Both areas are worth visiting but our circular walk is on the other side of the road – it goes through the old village of Shalfleet along Bridleways, lanes and over farmland to Newbridge Mill, and beside the Caul Bourne stream, back to the church.

Cross the main road from the inn and go down the lane opposite. Continue round, past the church, turning left when you reach the T-junction. Follow the road round a couple of bends until you reach a signed footpath on the right, no. S15 to Ningwood. Follow the path, at first through woods and then over the stile into the field. Bear right across to another stile and then left across to a gate in the corner of the field. Go out into the lane and turn left. A short distance ahead, on the right, is bridleway no. S16, turn right here (at one point the track briefly crosses the old disused railway line and runs along the edge of a field).

When you reach the Newbridge road go straight across, up the lane opposite turning left when you reach bridleway no. S22. Walk past Eade's Farm, down to the bottom of the track and take public footpath no. S42 on the right. Go into the field and, keeping close to the hedge on the left, walk round until you are level with a thatched cottage on the left; at this point go straight across the field

where you will find an opening in the hedge on the far side. The path winds its way through a small thicket then crosses the stream. Steps cut in the bank take you up to a short path; where it divides, go left, over the stile beside the gate, out into the road, and turn left.

As you round the bend, ignore the lane on the right, but go over the stile on to public footpath no. S35 (the path is well-trodden). On the far side go over the stile beside the gate, into the lane keeping straight ahead. After passing the farm and a couple of cottages the track goes off to the left, continue ahead down to a stile (public footpath no. 17). Go right, into the field. There is a well-defined path down to the stream, go into the adjoining field and continue round following the course of the stream, crossing the occasional bridge and stile. Eventually you reach a small green, ahead of you is a narrow grassy path which brings you out into the lane opposite the church, turn right back to the inn.

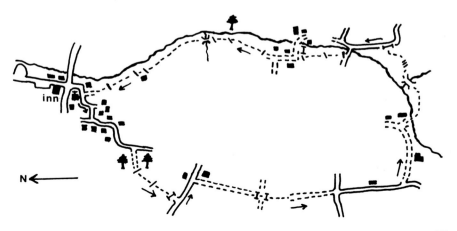

The Crown Inn, Shorwell

One of the loveliest pubs on the island, The Crown nestles beside a stream, opposite the church in the pretty village centre of Shorwell. It is an old inn, dating back to the 1600s and in its time it has been a staging post for coaches and, more secretively, a quiet retreat for smugglers. Today it is a very pleasant place to enjoy a meal or just sit beside the pretty trout stream, with a drink, watching the antics of the ducks and doves. The Crown is owned by Whitbreads and very well-run by the friendly tenants, Mike and Sally Grace. Two beautifully-kept bars have panelled walls, low-beamed ceilings and warm open log fires. The comfortable furnishings are an assortment of old tables, individual chairs and wooden wall settles – the larger bar has a lovely old dark oak dresser and there is a separate area where children may accompany their parents for a meal.

Real ale is still served traditionally straight from the barrel. You can choose from Flower's Original or Strong Country Bitter. For the summer months there is usually one extra beer such as Wethereds.

The inn is well-known locally for its excellent home-cooked food. From the set menu there are the usual snacks of ploughman's sandwiches and salads (the home-cooked gammon is delicious). Main meals include steak, home-made quiche, lasagne, chicken curry and 'Fisherman's pie' – white fish, prawns, peas and sweetcorn, in a white sauce topped with potato and cheese. The inn also offers a range of vegetarian dishes. Lunchtime and evening 'specials' are chalked on the blackboard. There is usually a soup, prawns, smoked trout or steak and kidney pie. One popular dish is chicken breast with apricot and brandy sauce served with sauté potatoes, vegetables or salad.

From May through till September the inn is open all day during the week from 11 a.m. till 11 p.m.; the rest of the year from 10.30 a.m. till 3 p.m. and 6 p.m. till 11 p.m.

Telephone: (0983) 740293.

Situated right in the centre of the village on the B3399.

Approx. distance of walk: 4¾ miles. O.S. Map No. 196 SZ 457/830.

The inn has two parking areas, one beside and one just past the garden.

A delightful scenic walk, fairly long but mostly dry and easy going. The first half takes you through the grounds of Wolverton Manor to the historic 18th-century Yafford Mill; the second half is a steep climb up onto Limerstone Down, more than compensated for by the glorious views. The route back to the inn is along the Worsely Trail and through the old part of the village.

Leave the inn and turn right towards Brighstone. Go up the hill past several private residences, until you come to a footpath (no. SW3). Go through the gate and bear right, across to another gate by the farm. Ahead of you is a similar gate; go through and turn left, down through one more gate, bearing right down to a stile at the bottom of the field. Go over and follow the narrow path over the brook and through the thicket, up towards Wolverton Manor (the path is fairly straightforward although it can be a bit wet). At the house bear right, go across the stream, bear right again, and go through the gate on the left, up through the farm to the lane and turn right. Continue walking until you reach the lane on the right to Yafford Mill. Turn here (If you wish to visit the mill it is open 10 a.m. to 6 p.m. from Easter till October).

The road passes between animal enclosures; when you reach the T-junction turn right, then turn left at the next junction, go up to the main road and turn left (on the right just past the farm is a signed bridleway no. S32). Go to the top, through the wooden gate and bear left, keeping to the right of the outcrop. The exact path is not entirely clear, but follow the sheep track up the down until you reach two gates, go through the one on the right, up and round the field, keeping to the fence on the left. At the top go through the small wooden gate and continue following the grass gully to the top of the down, turning right on the Worsley Trail (it is fairly long with two or three gates). When you eventually meet the road turn right, through the village back to the inn.

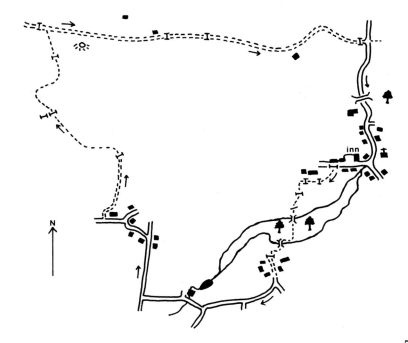

The Red Lion, Mortimer West End

Mortimer West End is a small village close to Silchester, where a Roman settlement flourished after the conquest of A.D. 43. The church of St Mary the Virgin dates from the 12th-century and stands on the site of two Roman temples; the north aisle is known as 'Mortimers Hole' because folk from Mortimer West End were allowed to worship there until their own parish church was opened. Three hundred metres to the west in the middle of the Roman town, hidden under the turf, is the earliest-known urban church north of the Alps.

Situated overlooking green fields, the Red Lion is a welcoming country pub dating from 1575. There is one attractive carpeted bar and a separate dining area. The ceilings are heavily beamed with more timber and part-wood panelling on the bare brick walls; at either end are large open fireplaces, one with a warm log fire in winter. At the front there are wooden seats on a sunny, sheltered terrace. The Red Lion is owned by Hall & Woodhouse. Four well kept real ales are served by handpump: they include Badger Best, Tanglefoot, Adnams Bitter and Wadsworth's 6X.

The main emphasis of this lovely pub must be the largely home-made food. There are the usual snacks such as ploughman's, quiche, salads and cottage pie but the speciality is their own home-made pies: there is seafood, chicken and mushroom, duck simmered in orange sauce and steak and kidney, braised in seasoned stock of Guinness and red wine – they are served in individual pots with a pastry topping accompanied by fresh vegetables and potatoes. Steak comes chargrilled or with a green pepper sauce. You can also have a tasty curry or chilli plus a couple of vegetarian dishes such as vegetable lasagne.

Children are very welcome. The inn is open during the week from 12 noon until 3 p.m. and again from 6 p.m. till 11 p.m.

Telephone: (0734) 700169.

Mortimer West End is a small village in the most northerly tip of Hampshire, about 5 miles north of Basingstoke. From the A30 at Pamber End, take the turning for Bramley and then the road to Silchester; it is all well signed.

Approx. distance of walk: 4 miles. O.S. Map No. 175 SU 633/635.

Park on either side of the inn.

A very interesting and most enjoyable walk in this lovely part of northern Hampshire. It is an easy walk, mostly good under foot with just a couple of muddy areas. The first half of the walk takes you through the lovely wooded, Benyon's Inclosure and across fishing lakes; the second half goes through the still un-excavated Roman town of Celleva. Sections of the perimeter wall are still standing and you also pass beside the amphitheatre which is in the process of excavation.

Leave the inn and turn right; just past the church cross over the road and go over the stile beside The Old School House. Follow the path down through the woods over the small bridge at the bottom and bear left over the wooden bridge and back up into the woods, keeping close to the field on the left. When you reach a gravel track turn right and almost immediately go left down the short path to meet a wider gravel track and turn left. Go across the lakes and turn right, following the track up into the woods until you reach the crossing point of a similar track; turn left here and left again when you reach the road.

Walk up to the T-junction and turn right on the road to Little London. Immediately bear left down Bramley Road, turning left again onto the bridleway just past the Roman museum. When you reach the stile beside the gate go over onto the path and continue ahead, through the small gate further on into Celleva.

Turn left, walk round and across to the far side, go through the small gate and bear right along the path to the church (it dates from the 12th-century). Go through the church-yard, out into the lane and turn left (on the corner of the road junction is the amphitheatre, a small gate allows you access). Continue straight ahead down the track; when you reach a stile on the left go into the field, and across in the direction of the electricity pylon.

At the bottom go over the stile, up the bank and the field ahead to a stile in the hedge at the top. Go over and turn left passing under the pylon and round the field to a crossing point beside the large oak. Continue ahead over one more stile and then go through the gate on the right, into the field and across to a small gate in the far left corner. Go through onto the track, turn left and then straight across the field, close to the hedge and out into the lane turning right. A short distance ahead is a bridleway on the right (it is not signed); go down to the bottom and turn right back up the hill to the inn.

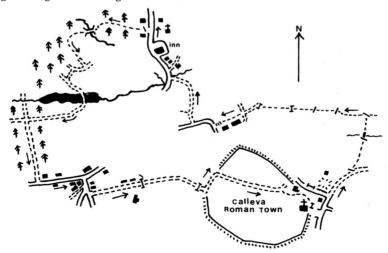

The Bush, Ovington

Hampshire is indeed fortunate having so many lovely unspoilt country inns like the Bush. Tucked away down a leafy lane, close to the River Itchen, it is hard to imagine that you are but minutes away from the busy A31. Inside the inn there are three cosy rooms served by the same bar; each has its own fireplace with a warm fire in winter and all around the dark walls are a wealth of old artefacts, brass and copper items, clocks, pictures, even a stuffed fish and enormous old bellows. The furnishings are a simple collection of elm tables, comfortable cushioned chairs and high-backed settles. Leading off the lower bar is a separate dining room; and there is seating in the attractive front garden. The inn is a freehouse very well run by the owners.

There are four real ales: Flower's Original, Wadsworth's 6X, Gale's H.S.B. and usually a guest beer such as Salisbury Best from Gibbs Mew.

One of the attractions of this lovely inn is its good food. There is an interesting bar menu with specials chalked daily on the blackboard. Snacks, apart from the usual sandwiches and ploughman's, include a tasty home-made soup such as creamy smoked salmon enhanced with brandy; there are oysters grilled in chilli, ginger, onion and soy sauce and 'Zakouski' – Russian cocktail of smoked salmon, prawns, grated cheese and red peppers. Main meals include grilled Itchen trout, halibut and lobster, scallops, prawns, haddock and mushrooms sauteéd in garlic butter served with a salad; there is Chateaubriand for two and the 'Bush Inn fillet' stuffed with stilton cheese, wrapped in bacon and served in a cream sauce. Daily specials might be beef, bacon and mushroom pie, or crispy chicken in a pineapple and celery sauce. Three vegetarian dishes include 'The Bush Pekinese stir fry'. The wine list is excellent – you should have no problem selecting a bottle you like from the 69 listed.

The inn is open during the week from 11 a.m. until 2.30 p.m. and from 6 p.m. till 11 p.m.

Telephone: (0962) 732764.

The village is signposted off the A31 between Winchester and Alresford. The inn is on the left at the bottom of the lane, close to the river.

Approx. distance of walk: 5¼ miles. O.S. Map No. 185 SU 561/318.

Park either in the inn's own car park or in the lane at the front.

A fairly long, but interesting walk which twice crosses the beautiful River Itchen. It takes you through the tranquil village of Avington with its Georgian church, goes across farmland, through woods and along peaceful country lanes.

From the inn turn left and immediately go down the footpath on the left beside the inn. Go over the wooden bridge across the Itchen and bear left, following the gravel path until you reach another bridge on the right. Go over, up the lane to the road, and turn left. Continue walking through Itchen Stoke village, past several dwellings, turning left onto a gravel track just past River's Keep cottage (the footpath is signed). Walk down to the stile beside the gate, go into the field and straight across to a small stone bridge. Continue ahead over the wooden bridge, across the Itchen, and bear right, then left, over another bridge, following the path until you come to a stile on the right. Go over into the field and across to the stile on the far side, keeping fairly close to the hedge on the right. Continue ahead across the field making for a stile in the hedge beside the house. Walk round onto the front drive, then up to the lane and turn right.

After a short distance you will reach a stile on the left. Bear right up the field, over the stile in the fence and turn left. Further on you will see a track off to the right leading into a clump of trees (it is signed);

turn right here and then straight on at the cross tracks keeping a line of yew trees on your right, turning right at the end down to the lane. Turn left and keep straight on, through the village of Avington (The unspoilt Georgian church dates from 1770 and is one of the most perfect in the country). The lane is long but eventually leads down to Avington Manor Farm. On the left, just past the farm, is a signed bridleway. Go through the double wooden gates up into Hampage Wood. At the top the bridleway branches in several directions; take the small path on the left in front of the house just to the right of the wire fence (do not go along the wide forest track). The path enters the perimeter of the woods, winding its way through for some distance, before emerging out into a quiet lane (it is very attractive but can become a bit overgrown in the summer and a bit muddy in winter). Turn right, go along the lane to the T-junction, and turn left back to the inn.

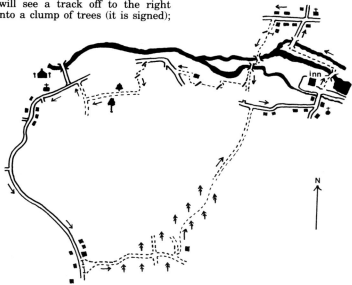

The Ship Inn, Owslebury

The Ship Inn, originally called the Britannia, dates back to 1681 and was used as recently as 1900 for the customary Court of Marwell Manor, who met for the conduct of such business as came within its concern. It was once thatched but now has a tiled and rendered front. The one main attractive bar has a lovely atmosphere: there is a central fireplace with an open fire in the winter and, in one corner, a dartboard. The rest of the bar has simple seating with polished tables and all round are dozens of ship's timbers serving as wall and beam props. On the other side of the entrance porch is a separate family room and at the rear an attractive lawned beer garden with picnic benches and children's play area, with lovely views towards Winchester.

The inn is owned by Marston's and well run by the licensee, Robert O'Neill.

There are three real ales: Marston's Pedigree, Burton and Merrie Monk.

Food is served six days a week (not Sundays), from 12 noon till 2 p.m. and again, from 7 p.m. till 9 p.m. (9.30 p.m. on Friday and Saturday). There is plenty of choice from basket meals and jacket potatoes to sandwiches and ploughman's; Other snacks include smoked salmon, prawn fritters, smoked trout and the 'Ship's platter' – breaded mushrooms, cougons of plaice, breaded courgettes and butterfly prawns served with brown bread and garlic mayonnaise. For a main meal you can choose smoked chicken or breaded plaice, various grills or one of the home-made specialities, such as beef in red wine, chilli-con-carne, vegetable curry or spaghetti bolognese. To complete your meal there is a good selection of sweets and a varied wine list which includes some from France and Australia.

The inn is open during the week from 11 a.m. till 2.30 p.m. and again from 6 p.m. through till 11 p.m. (10.30 p.m. in winter).

Telephone: (0962) 74358.

Owslebury is a very pretty peaceful village yet only minutes away from the busy Winchester by-pass. It is best reached from the south turning off the B2177, between Fisher's Pond and Bishop's Waltham. If approaching from the north, either take the turning off the A272 or the turning for Twyford at the end of the Winchester by-pass: a couple of miles further on take the turning on the right, just past four silver grain silos. Owslebury is not signed but just keep straight ahead until you reach the village.

Approx. distance of walk: 3½ miles. O.S. Map No. 185 SU 234/512.

The inn has its own large car park, and there is also a small crescent in front used for parking.

An easy walk through delightful countryside on well-established paths and tracks. Although it can be a little muddy in places, it is ideal for the whole family, especially as it passes through woods on the outskirts of the well-known Marwell Zoological Park.

Leave the inn and turn right; a few steps further on take the drive on the left (it is signed 'Longfield'). Just before reaching the entrance to the house take the narrow tree-lined path on the left; it is a lovely path edged with bluebells, quite long and can be a bit muddy. When you reach a path crossing, turn left and follow it past bluebell woods on the left, over a gravel track, and ahead up into woods. At the top you come out onto a gravel track with the Marwell Zoo car-park on the right. Keep straight ahead following the bridlepath which brings you out by the entrance to the park. Walk straight across the road and follow the signed bridlepath ahead into a narrow strip of woodland, and then, before reaching the road, turn immediately left. Follow the path through the trees, across a small area of open grassland and back into the woods. Keep close to the perimeter fence, at one point crossing a track back into the woods on the other side. When you reach the wire fence, bordering a

field, turn left walking down and round past Marwell Hall and the animal enclosures.

Just before you reach the road follow the bridlepath on the left, up round the enclosure, and eventually out into the road. Turn left just before reaching Whaddon Farm, go up the short track on the right (the footpath is signed but concealed in the overgrown hedge). Go over the wooden crossing point, into the field, and straight ahead keeping close to the hedge on the left. When you reach a large open field bear left, following the hedge up, and round to a gate in the top corner. Go through and up the track until you reach the church at the top. Go left up the steps, through the churchyard and out through the front gate, turning left back to the inn.

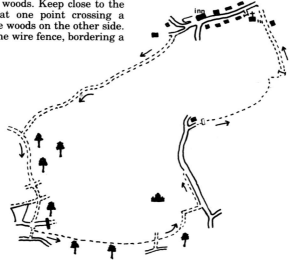

July 16, 2005
Emma, Susan, William,
Peter, Tina, Ann +
andy
Reeve

The Chequers Inn, Pennington

The Chequers, a lovely unspoilt inn close to the sea and in a peaceful rural lane dates originally from the 16th-century and was once the local salt exchange. It is a charming inn bursting with character. The welcoming interior is simply furnished with comfortable chairs, various old tables and wall pews on the part-tiled and boarded floor and is partly heated by a warm wood-burning stove. Children are allowed in a separate area away from the bar and also in the restaurant. Outside is a central court-yard with a summer barbecue and picnic benches. The inn is a freehouse well-run by licensees, Michael and Maggie Jamieson.

There are four well-kept real ales: Wadsworth's 6X, Flower's Original, Strong Country Bitter plus a guest ale, such as Ringwood Bitter, Burton Ale or Fullers London Pride.

Good food is available both lunchtimes and in the evenings, the menu being chalked on the blackboard in the main bar. There are the usual pub favourites like ploughman's and home-made soup. Seafood naturally features strongly: well-presented seafood salad consists of prawns, tuna and crab meat on a bed of mixed salad garnished with whole prawns and mussels; you can also choose seafood lasagne or fresh whole plaice. If, like me, you enjoy garlic bread the Chequers serve it topped with prawns and melted cheese. Other dishes include chilli or grilled chops with a barbecue sauce. To complete your meal there are several tempting sweets, steamed ginger pudding and banana split, to name but two. A more comprehensive menu is available in the restaurant.

Dogs are allowed, but not in the evening at week-ends. Opening times during the week are flexible but generally from 11 a.m. until 2.30 p.m. and again from 6 p.m. till 11 p.m.

Telephone: (0590) 673415.

From the A337 at Pennington go down to the bottom of Ridgway Lane; the inn is on the right.

Approx. distance of walk: 4½ miles. O.S Map No. 196 SU 322/936.

Park at the front of the inn.

A bracing coastal walk along the Solent Way. It is easy going, ideal for the whole family partly across open fields, along country lanes and on gravel tracks.

Leave the inn and turn right; immediately turn right again into the private road (the footpath is signed). Walk past a couple of houses and before reaching the entrance to Pennington House, go over the stile to the right of a private residence (it is signed). Follow the path up to a second stile and into the field ahead. Keeping close to the hedge, walk across to the far side, go through the gap in the hedge on the right, into the adjoining field and turn left. Keeping close to the hedge on the left, continue across the far side, over the stile, into the lane and turn left.

After a short distance you come to a metal gate on the right (the footpath is signed). Turn right here and follow the track until you reach a stile, go over onto the grassy track and continue ahead until you reach the road. Walk straight across, go over the stile onto the gravel track, and turn left. It is fairly long, winding its way past several fields, and between quarries, before reaching a stile. Go over into the lane and turn right to Keyhaven.

As you reach the car park you will see a signed footpath on the left running beside the sea wall. Turn left here and follow the footpath along the length of shoreline, past Pennington Marshes and historic salt beds. When you reach a small jetty turn left, go through the wooden gate and follow the gravel track inland, through two more gates, turning right when you reach the lane. After several hundred yards you will see a signed footpath on the right; turn right here. It winds its way past several houses; a gate then gives access to a country lane. Follow it round until you reach the inn.

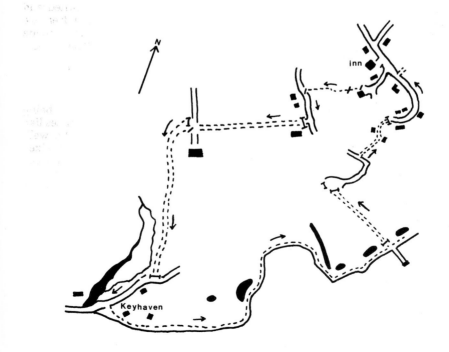

The Fleur-de-Lys Inn, Pilley

Sometimes during my walks I come across an inn I've not visited before, but it is rare to find a local inn as old and as charming as The Fleur-de-Lys, that I have to admit was previously unknown to me. In the entrance passageway is a list of all the landlords since 1498 although beer is believed to have been sold here since 1096. Originally the inn was a pair of forester's cottages; the tree roots and fireplace opening (an old New Forest Rights tradition) can still be seen in the stone flagged entrance passage. The inn was described in Sir Arthur Conan-Doyle's book 'The White Company'. There are two bars: the public bar and the lounge both named after characters from the book 'The Children of the New Forest' which was written in the locality. The lounge is very attractive with a heavy-beamed ceiling and the walls covered with old artefacts, copper and antique brass items. At one end is a beautiful large inglenook fireplace where, until a few years ago, ham was still smoked in the chimney (the chain and pulley at the chimney head are still there); in the winter there is a roaring log fire. The furnishings are simple comfortable chairs and farmhouse tables. The inn also has a separate attractive restaurant again with a large open fireplace, a small family room and a pretty garden at the back with picnic benches.

Real ale is still served traditionally, straight from the barrel. There is usually a choice from either Flower's Original, Marston's Pedigree and Pompey Royal.

Hot and cold snacks are available from the bar menu, plus several daily specials chalked on the blackboard. A good choice of starters include home-made soup, garlic mushrooms with prawns and cheese, and pate; Followed by lasagne, crispy cod or a home-made curry. Snacks, such as sandwiches and ploughman's, are also available and a much more comprehensive table-de-hote menu can be found in the restaurant.

The inn is open during the week from 11 a.m. until 2.30 p.m. (3 p.m. on Saturdays), and from 6 p.m. till 10.30 p.m.

Telephone: (0590) 72158.

Pilley is a small village close to the Lymington River; it can be reached either from the B3054 or the A337 Brockenhurst to Lymington road.

Approx. distance of walk: 2¾ miles. O.S. Map No. 196 SZ 327/983.

Parking is rather limited to a small pull-in beside the inn or the road itself.

A short but very enjoyable walk on country lanes, through woods and along the banks of the Lymington River. It is easy going, mostly dry – ideal for a warm summer's evening. For a longer walk you can, if you wish, combine this walk with the Hobler at Battramsley; both walks cross at The Red Lion in Boldre.

Leave the inn turning left and immediately go over the stile behind the pull-in. Continue ahead, over the stile in front of you and straight across the field to the stile on the far side, go out into the lane and turn right. When you reach the T-junction, turn left and continue along the road until you reach a bridleway on the right, just before the bend in the road, beside Southlands School; it takes you down towards Vicar's Hill Farm. At the end of the lane go down between the houses, over the concrete drive and down the path to the river; at the bottom you will see the path goes to the right (it is signed). It is regularly walked and not too difficult to follow, but is inclined to become a bit overgrown in summer. On the far side is

a small wooden gate which leads you out onto a gravel track, turn left, cross the bridge, walk up to the road junction and turn right.

At the T-junction in Boldre turn right unless you are combining both walks, in which case turn left, and then go down the lane opposite The Red Lion (turn to Page 7). (turn to Page 7) Continue down the hill, over the bridge turning left into Rodlease Rough herb nursery, turn right and go up the track until you reach a signed footpath on the right. Follow it down into the woods, through and out into the lane turning right. Go up to the T-junction at Pilley Hill and then turn right back to the inn.

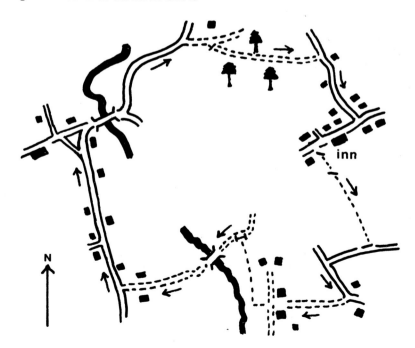

N

inn

The White Horse ('The Pub with No Name'), Priors Dean

The White Horse, as it does not have an inn sign, is often referred to as 'The Pub With No Name'. It is a lovely inn, remotely situated and surrounded by cornfields built in the 17th-century – a fact which becomes obvious once you are inside. The atmosphere is relaxed and un-hurried, one of the reasons for its popularity. The two attractive bars have low beamed ceilings and real log fires. The beautiful old fireplace in the main bar extends the whole length of the end wall. All the walls are adorned with a large collection of memorabilia, pictures, old clocks, farm implements, old brass and copper items, etc. the wall coverings themselves have attained a rich warm patina only associated with age. Outside there is a secluded beer garden and a small front terrace with picnic benches. The inn is a freehouse very well run by the friendly owners.

The range of real ales, usually a dozen or so, is excellent: there is Huntsman's Royal Oak, Ringwood's Forty-niner, King and Barnes Sussex Bitter and their draught Mild, Gale's H.S.B., No Name Bitter (King and Barnes 'Festive'), Bass, Ballard's Bitter and Courage Best; there is also usually a guest beer. For those who like country wines a good choice is available, tapped straight from china kegs.

The food list is not large, but it is very good: the usual bar snacks include ploughman's, sandwiches (both plain and toasted), home-made soup and salads. Every day there are two or three hot dishes listed on the blackboard: these could be chicken masala, Lancashire hot pot, or chicken, gammon and mushroom pie; seafood lasagne consists of layers of natural lasagne duglere, cream and tomato sauce with mixed seafood and mushrooms, topped with bechamel and grated cheese.

The inn is open during the week from 11 a.m. till 2.30 p.m. (3 p.m. at weekends), and in the evening from 6 p.m. (7 p.m. on Sunday) till 11 p.m.

Telephone: (042 058) 387.

A difficult inn to find! From Petersfield take the A272; just beyond the railway station, turn right at the roundabout towards Steep. Keep to the main road until you reach the East Tisted/Privett cross roads and turn right; take the second proper track on the right. Alternatively the inn can be reached from Alton or Winchester on the A32.

Approx. distance of walk: 4¾ miles. O.S. Map No. 197 SU 714/290.

Park in the large gravel car park in front of the inn or in the track.

A lovely peaceful country walk, quite hilly in places but easy going. It is mostly on country lanes and established tracks with a small section on farmland. It is best walked during fine weather; it can be extremely muddy.

From the car park go into the field in front of the inn, across to the stile opposite; go over and turn left. Keeping close to the hedge continue along to another stile, go out into the lane and turn right, further on, where the lane forks, go to the right and follow it round, ignoring a right turn until you come up to a T-junction. Take the track on the right going past the farm and out into the lane at the far end. Turn left, walk up to the T-junction and turn right. After a few steps you will come to a footpath on the left (it is signed). Go down this path, steeply at first, to the lane at the bottom and turn right.

The hill is quite steep, a 1-in-5 gradient. At the bottom, before you reach the road junction, is a track on the right. Turn right here, walking past the house and up the path ahead (it is very steep and can be quite muddy). It eventually merges with Warren Lane before reaching the road at the top. Go straight across the road, over the stile opposite and across the field, keeping close to the hedge on the left. At one point, where the hedge goes left, continue straight ahead picking it up again on the far side of the field. The path widens to a grassy track as it passes beside farm buildings; it then bears to the right. In the hedge on the left is a signed footpath – turn left here. Keep close to the wooden fence and then go straight down across the middle of the field in the far hedge. Cross over into the smaller field and bear left back to the inn.

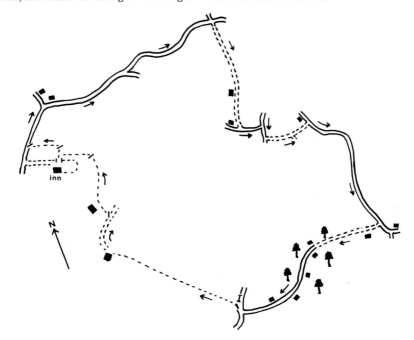

The Rose and Thistle Inn, Rockbourne

Rockbourne must surely be one of the prettiest villages in Hampshire – a small brook runs the entire length of the winding village street which is strung with beautiful thatched cottages and lovely old period houses. At one end is the Rose and Thistle, a very attractive thatched, white painted two-storey inn, set back from the road with a pretty front garden. Originally two cottages it first became an inn about 180 years ago. Inside there are two bars, both different, but both full of character: one was actually two small rooms, now divided by a couple of timber props; the ceiling is part-plastered and part-boarded, with each end of the bar having its own distinctive fireplace. The furniture is a lovely assortment of old pine and oak tables, wooden settles, and cut-down barrels. The other bar is dominated by an enormous old inglenook fireplace with a roaring log fire in the winter; beside the hearth is a high-backed wooden settle and a small tip top circular table. More cushioned high and low-backed settles are separated by wooden props, supporting the heavy beamed and close-boarded ceiling; all around the walls are various old pictures and polished brass. The front garden, with a small thatched dove cote, has several wooden benches.

Two real ales are available, Strong Country Bitter and Pompey Royal. White wine from the Loire and Burgundy feature strongly on the wine list which also includes reds and wine from Germany and Italy.

The inn is well-known locally for its fresh seafood, especially lobster and crab salads; other fish regularly on the menu are salmon, Dover and lemon sole. Besides fish there are salads of beef and home-cooked Wiltshire ham, home-made steak and kidney pie and venison in season, prime steak and vegetarian dishes.

You can, of course, just have a ploughman's or a sandwich if you prefer.

The inn is open during the week from 11 a.m. till 3 p.m. and from 6 p.m. till 11.30 p.m. Dogs or children are not allowed inside the pub.

Telephone: (07253) 236.

66

From the A338 at Fordingbridge take the B3078 towards Damerham; the turning for Rockbourne is well signed. The inn is on the left at the far end of the village.

Approx. distance of walk: 3 miles. O.S. Map No. 184 SU 115/184.

Park behind the inn.

The most westerly walk in the book, a good one for all seasons but best walked on a fine day. It is interesting throughout – crossing farmland, going down country lanes and through woods.

Leave the inn and turn right. Almost immediately walk up the lane on the left past the church, left through the gates and round to the back of the farm. Go over the cattle grid on the left into the field, and follow the track up and round to the right, over another grid and continue ahead (ignore the track off to the left). A metal gate eventually gives you access to a country lane. Turn left and straight ahead at the crossroads to the top of the hill. Almost opposite the pond, and close to a letterbox, a footpath leads off into woods on the right. Turn right here and where the path divides take the right fork down through a bluebell wood. When you reach the road walk straight across and go up the footpath to the right of the house.

It winds its way through woodland before emerging out onto a gravel farm track. Turn right and, a few steps further on, go into the field on the left. Walk straight across and make for a stile in the far corner. Go down the embankment, onto the gravel track and turn right (you will see a monument on the hill on the left, it was erected to the memory of Sir Eyre Coote). When you reach the road go straight across, over the stile and across to the farm. Go right through the wooden gate, down beside the house and out through another gate into the lane. Almost opposite is a stile leading into a field. Keeping close to the hedge on the right, continue across turning right when you reach a farm track, and then go immediately left into the adjoining field. Keep close to the hedge, walking across until you reach a gap in the corner of the field. Go through, across the rear lawns of several cottages, over the stile onto a small village green. Ahead of you is a gravel drive, follow it left down to the village and turn right back to the inn.

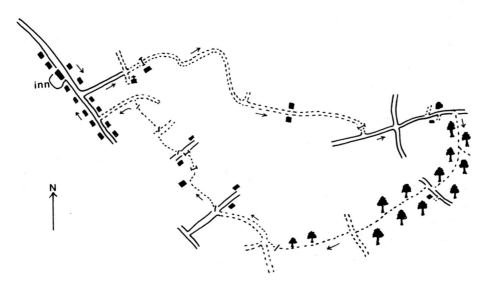

N

The Coach and Horses, Rotherwick

The residents of Rotherwick are very lucky having an inn as good as the Coach and Horses. It is a freehouse, very efficiently run by the licensee Mrs Terry Hall, which dates back to the 16th-century. It has been altered over the years without losing its character. The two attractively furnished bars have open fireplaces with warm log fires in winter. At the rear of the inn is a separate dining room and outside at the front, several picnic benches, surrounded by tubs of flowers in summer.

Rarely in my travels have I found a country inn offering such a large range of well-kept real ales: during most of the year you can choose from at least nine, plus a couple of specials, to as many as fifteen in December. Typically there is Theakston Old Perculier, Ringwood's Old Thumper, Fuller's London Pride, Palmer's Best, Marston's Pedigree, Badger Best, Royal Oak and I.P.A. from Eldridge Pope, even the very strong Owd Roger. Regular guest beers include Bateman's Victory, Smiles Exhibition and Arkells Kingsdown.

Food is served seven days a week with a carvery on Sunday – booking is essential. The menu is chalked daily on the blackboard. Various snacks include sandwiches, ploughman's and usually a tasty soup. The inn is well-known for its good range of home-made pizzas. Other bar meals available can be chilli, smoked trout pate, and home-made beefburgers; there is often a special such as bubble and squeak with cold meats or perhaps a rabbit pie. Main meals include a choice of grills, home-made steak and kidney and a seafood platter. A small but good wine list offers four French reds plus white and house wine.

Children are welcome in the areas away from the bar. The inn is open during the week from 11 a.m. until 2.30 p.m. and again from 5.30 p.m. till 10.30 p.m.

Telephone: (025 672) 2542.

Rotherwick lies to the east of Basingstoke between the A33 and the A30. From the M3 come off at junction 5, take the A287 to Newnham and then the road to Rotherwick, turning right when you reach the village, the inn is just past the church on the right.

Approx. distance of walk: 3¾ miles. O.S. Map Nos. 175 and 186 SU 713/563.

Park in the inn's own car park or beside the verge at the front.

An enjoyable walk across farmland, through woods and along peaceful country lanes. It is fairly easy going, mostly on dry level ground.

Leave the inn and turn right. A short distance later take the signed footpath on the right. Keep straight ahead, at first following the track beside the hedge, and then across the open field, bearing left on the far side, out onto the gravel track and turn left. When you reach the road turn right. Continue for a couple of hundred yards looking for a footpath on the left (there is a small post painted with a yellow arrow). Turn left here following it through the woods, out into a field, and ahead, keeping close to the hedge on the left. A gap in the hedge gives you access to the field ahead. Go through and immediately turn left, keeping close to the hedge, follow the path back into, and straight through the woods to the stile beside the road.

Walk straight across and follow the signed footpath beside the woods. Go over the stile and continue ahead until you emerge into a small clearing. Turn left, walk past the houses, straight across the lane and down the track towards Wedman's Farm. After passing through a gate you will see a signed footpath on the left beside the brick garage. Turn left here and follow the path down to a stile, go over into the field and turn right. Walk round, keeping close to the hedge. When you reach a wooden crossing point, go into the adjoining field and turn left. Go over the stile ahead of you and across the field to a metal gate in the far hedge. Continue ahead up the field to a stile behind the large oak. Go across into the field, and keeping close to the hedge on the left, walk to the far side, go out through the gate and turn right.

At the Fox inn turn left, walk down and round the lane, past woodland on the left, until you reach an opening into the field (the footpath is signed). Turn left and walk round, keeping to the path beside the hedge until you come to a farm track. Turn left, walk down to the road, go across on to the track opposite and through the farm back to the inn.

N

Susan, William, Dec. 15, 2006
Peter, Tina

The Woolpack, Sopley

In the middle of Sopley village, beside a tributary of the River Avon, sits the pretty Woolpack Inn. The two-storey thatched pub dates from around the middle of the 18th-century. During the last war it was a popular meeting place for the aircrew stationed nearby at R.A.F. Sopley. Various alterations have been carried out since that time, but the character of the original inn still remains. There is now one main bar with a low beamed ceiling and open log fires. At the side of the inn is a large conservatory which provides additional dining space. Outside at the front and beside the stream, are wall-partitioned seating areas, where on a fine day it is a very pleasant place to sit and watch the antics of the ducks.

The inn has a well-stocked bar offering three real ales – Ringwood Bitter, Wadsworth 6X and Marston's Pedigree.

The Woolpack is a very popular place to eat and can be very busy especially at lunchtimes and weekends. There are the usual bar snacks such as sandwiches, ploughman's lunch, filled jacket potatoes and quiche. Also several hot dishes such as a tasty curry and cottage pie. A very good restaurant menu offers a range of starters which include Indonesian pork sate, and moules mariniere. There is a choice of steaks, escalope of veal, rack of lamb and fish dishes including fillet of halibut in a mussel butter sauce.

There is a separate children's menu and vegetarians are catered for.

The inn is now open all day during the week.

Telephone: (0425) 72252.

Sopley can be reached either from Ringwood or Christchurch on the B3347. It is approximately 5½ miles from Ringwood.

Approx. distance of walk: 4½ miles. O.S. Map No. 195 SZ 156/969.

There is a large car park beside the inn, alternatively park in the road opposite which leads to the church.

A very pleasant country walk, flat, easy going, mostly dry and ideal for the whole family. It follows the course of a stream, crosses farmland and goes along country tracks.

Leave the inn and turn right in the direction of Ringwood. Just past Sopley forge, but before reaching a new house, you will see a stile on the right. Go over onto the footpath, following the course of the stream, in springtime it is dotted with bluebells). After a while you reach a stile, go over into the field and straight ahead, keeping close to the hedge on the right. You will eventually reach another stile on the right which will take you along the riverbank and up to a stile beside a bridge. Go straight across the lane and follow the footpath ahead, beside the stream. A short distance further on a stile will give you access to a large field. Continue ahead to another stile, and cross

the road (the footpath is well marked). A short grassy path leads to a stile which takes you into a large field. Continue ahead following the course of the stream until you come to a wooden crossing point on the right. Go through and follow the path round to the left and then right over the concrete bridge into the small field and straight ahead up to the lane.

When you reach the road junction turn left, then immediately right, through the metal gate on to the grassy track (it is fairly long and at one point crosses the stream). When you eventually reach a wooden gate go through onto the gravel track and follow it round to the right, out through another

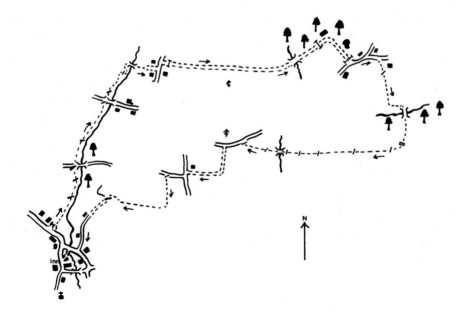

The sketch maps in this book are not necessarily to scale but have been drawn to show the maximum amount of detail.

gate into the lane, and turn left. A few steps later take the right fork. You will see a signed footpath leading into a copse on the right. Go through and over a stile opposite into a large field. Keeping close to the hedge on the right, go straight over to the far side and then follow the hedge to the left until you come to an opening on the right. The small bridge will take you across the stream and into the field. When you reach the far right-hand corner, go over the wooden crossing point and then over the stile on the right into the field (the path is well signed). Walk round the field, keeping close to the hedge on the right. When you reach the far side go over the stile and continue ahead over a couple more stiles until you enter a small thicket. On the far side is a stile and a wooden bridge crossing the stream.

Continue ahead over one more stile and into the field, ignore the stile on the right but continue round the field until eventually reaching a stile beside a gate leading out into a country lane. Turn left and, after only a short distance, take the track on the left. It is fairly long but keep going until it reaches a crossroads. Go over and down the lane opposite. When you reach a stile on the left, go into the field and follow the path around the perimeter until you find one last stile set in the hedge on the left. It gives you access to a narrow wooded track which eventually merges into a quiet country lane. When you come to the one-way system, turn right, go over the road and take the little concrete bridge over the river turning left, back to the inn.

Walk No. 18   Walk No. 39

Two Interesting Inn Signs

The Village Duck Pond, Crawley, Walk No. 8

The Picturesque Village of East Stratton, Walk No. 13

The Plough Inn, Sparsholt

The Plough is an ideal finish to an enjoyable family walk: there is a good public bar and a comfortable lounge heated by a log fire in winter. Outside there is a small attractive terrace and a large beer garden with a children's play-area and hut. The Plough was originally a farmhouse built between two and three hundred years ago. It is now owned by Whitbread's and well-run by the friendly tenants, Andy and Linda Paterson.

Three regular real ales include Flower's Original, Pompey Royal and a guest beer.

Meals are served in the pub from 12 noon to 2 p.m. daily and 7 p.m. to 9 p.m., Wednesday to Sunday evenings. You can choose from the bar menu, the blackboard specials or from the more extensive a-la-carte list; a separate children's menu is available from the bar. The food is very good, most of it home-made. Soups are a speciality, a different one chosen each day from some twenty available such as crab chowder, cheese and vegetables and salmon bisque. Other snacks include jacket potatoes, imaginative ploughman's and freshly cut plain or toasted sandwiches. For your main meal you could choose seafood lasagne, chicken kiev, whole lemon sole, breaded and stuffed with crab meat, or a jumbo steak and kidney pie – over half a pound of meat topped with home-made short crust pastry. Vegetarians are well catered for with spinach and walnut lasagne, macaroni cheese, a vegetable chilli and sometimes a special, such as courgette and cheese quiche. To accompany your meal the wine list offers some 21 reasonably priced wines.

The inn is open during the week from 10.30 a.m. until 2.30 p.m. and again from 6 p.m. till 11 p.m.

Telephone: (096 272) 353.

Situated to the west of Winchester, Sparsholt can be reached either from the A3090 in the south, or the A272 in the north.

Approx. distance of walk: 5½ miles. O.S. Map No. 185 SU 439/314.

The inn has its own large car park.

Sparsholt is a small, quaint, peaceful village yet only four miles from the busy M3. It is a delightful walk, easy going on established bridlepaths, through woods, across farmland and down quiet country lanes. It also passes through Farley Mount Country Park. Whilst you will encounter the odd muddy patch the going is mostly dry.

Turn right from the inn and go down Home Lane, opposite Corner cottage. When you reach the T-junction turn right, turning left at the next bend. The lane goes down and round to a farm at the bottom. Bear right, between farm buildings, out onto the tarmac drive beyond. Follow this drive for just over half a mile until you reach a signed bridleway on the left, almost opposite a pair of green farm buildings. Go left into the field following the track across to a second field, then bear slightly to the left to pick up the track again and continue ahead. The field narrows to meet woodland on the far side; you will see a small wooden gate. Go through into West Wood and follow the track straight ahead (ignoring the side tracks), until you reach a wooden half gate on the far side of the woods. go through onto

the gravel track out onto open grassland and bear left by a line of logs. There is a well-defined track which will take you up through Farley Mount Country Park and out into the lane beside the car park, at the top.

Turn left, walking until you reach a signed bridleway on the left next to a Forestry Commission entrance. Turn left here and follow the path through the woods, ignoring the side turnings, until the path merges with a gravel driveway. Walk down to the road, go straight across, down the gravel track, and follow the footpath ahead until you reach a track on the left. Turn left here, walking down to meet the road at Dean. Go left up the hill, and left again at the T-junction, back to the inn.

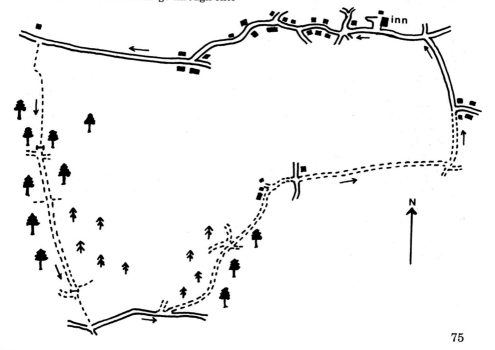

The Harrow, Steep

The Harrow at Steep is a very quaint, two-storey, brick-and-tiled inn tucked peacefully away close to the county border with West Sussex. It was once an old coaching stop, enjoyed by today's motorists in much the same way as those bygone travellers. Inside there are two small simply furnished bars, one has a large inglenook fireplace with an open log fire in the winter. Outside, at the front, is a sunny terrace with lots of wooden tables and benches. There is more seating to the side in a lovely unspoilt garden. The inn is a Whitbread house, run by Eddy and Ellan McCutcheon.

Well-kept real ales are tapped straight from the barrels at the back of the small servery. There are three to choose from: Flower's Original, Strong Country and Boddington's Bitter. Traditional cider and country wines are also available.

The food list is small but very good – everything is home-made on the premises. Snacks include a tasty soup, ploughman's lunches and salads of home-cooked ham, cheese, rare beef, excellent home-made meat loaf and scotch eggs. Other hot meals include lasagne, cauliflower cheese and shepherd's pie.

Children are not allowed in either of the bars. Opening times during the week are from 11 a.m. in the morning till 2.30 p.m. (3 p.m. at weekends) and from 6 p.m. till 11 p.m.

Telephone: (0730) 62685.

From Petersfield, the village of Steep is well signposted from either the A272 or the A325. The inn is in a small lane not far from the church – look for the inn sign above the hedge.

Approx. distance of walk: 3½ miles. O.S. Map No. 197 SU 752/252.

Parking is limited at the inn, there are several spaces opposite plus some room in the lane outside.

A most enjoyable short walk in this beautiful part of east Hampshire. It is quite hilly but fairly dry underfoot. The walk goes through woods, across farmland and down tranquil country lanes.

Leave the inn and turn left. Go down to the bottom of the lane, over the woooden foot-bridge, and follow the path left past the cottage and up into the woods. When you emerge on to a country lane, turn left, go past a few houses until you reach a stile on the left beside a farm gate. Go over, up the track, and over another stile into the field ahead. Keeping close to the fence on the right, walk down to the bottom; go through the wire fence and down to meet a track.

Turn right, go over the stile and into the woods (the path is well-defined, eventually bringing you out onto the lawn of a private house). Go straight across, to the left of the house, and back into woods (the path is well signed and brings you out close to farm buildings). Walk round to the left and up to a wooden crossing point in the corner. Keeping close to the hedge on the right, walk down to the far side of the field and through the gap in the corner; go over the wooden crossing point and up the path ahead until you reach a stile in the wire fence on the right. Cross over into the adjoining field and continue walking up until you reach a point where the footpath has been diverted. Instead of walking ahead up to the farm, you now have to go to the right round the field (it is well signed).

When you come to a stile on the left, to the right of a farm gate, go across and up the path until you reach the lane at the top; then turn left. At first it is level then descends quite steeply. As you near the bottom, there is a farm on the left; turn down between the main building and the calf pens and follow the farm road to the bottom. Do not go over the wooden bridge but turn right into the field (there is a foot path marker on the tree), and make your way across to the far right-hand corner, over the stile and into the woods. The path is well-marked eventually bringing you out onto the lawn opposite the church. Go out into the lane and turn left, walking down and round for about half a mile, turning left when you reach the crossroads, back to the inn.

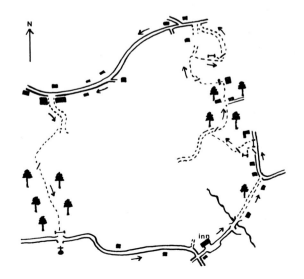

The Mayfly, Testcombe

The best thing about The Mayfly is the glorious river-side setting. It is very much a commercial inn with a fast, efficient food service. Owned by Whitbreads and run by Julie and Barry Lane, it is comfortably furnished and nicely decorated with various fishing regalia around the walls. In winter the bars are heated by open wood-burning stoves. Outside there are lots of picnic benches beside the river.

The inn offers two real ales: Flower's Original and Whitbread's Strong Country; also on draught is Whitbreads 1% low alcohol beer.

Food is ordered and collected from a separate counter. The choice from the menu is limited but there are always a couple of specials chalked on the blackboard: you can start with soup, a choice of cheeses or "hot" quiche a-la-maison; there are various cold meat salads plus hot chicken tandoori. Special dishes can be slices of local river trout or half a smoked chicken. Various puddings are listed on the board behind the food bar.

If you are back late from your walk, don't worry, the inn is open all day Monday to Saturday from 11 a.m. till 11 p.m. Food is only served between 12 noon and 2 p.m. (Sunday 2.30 p.m.) and from 7 p.m. to 9 p.m.

Telephone: (026474) 283.

The inn is situated on the B3057 between Stockbridge and Andover.

Approx. distance of walk: 4 miles. O.S. Map No. 185 SU 382/391.

The inn has its own large car park; there is also a public parking area by West Down on the road to Chilbolton.

A beautiful scenic walk through the pretty Test Valley – it is one of my favourites. It crosses both the Test and Anton rivers, goes over farmland and along country lanes. It is an easy walk, well-marked, fairly dry underfoot, ideal for the whole family; there is just one hilly section where a little care is necessary.

From the inn turn right, go over the bridge and turn left on the road to Chilbolton – take care as the road can be busy. (If you want to avoid this section of the road and extend the walk, you can take the Test Way on the right up onto West Down, following the signs round and back down to the road nearer the village). Otherwise continue ahead until you reach a small enclosed green with a seat and horse-chesnut tree on the left. Take the signed footpath walking down towards the river (the path is easy to follow). When you emerge out into a playing field, keep to the left round the field until you come to a small path leading up to a

stile. Go over and turn right to meet a gravel track (in very wet weather it would be advisable to continue round the field and go out through the metal gate directly onto the track). Follow the track past a cottage, turning left when you meet a similar track. Cross the stream and then take the footpath on the left up to and over the bridge, then straight ahead across the meadow. On the far side is another small bridge, go across, along the path, across another bridge, up and out into the lane.

Turn left. Walk past several cottages (ignoring the signed footpath on the right), until you reach a signed bridleway on the

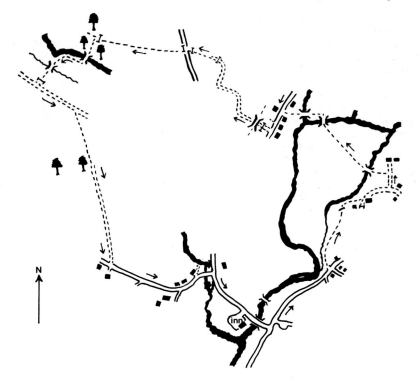

right. Go through the gate and under the bridge following the grassy track up and round the fields. At one point the path goes through a wooden gate and then down towards the road; at the bottom go through the gate, across the road, through the gate and onto the bridleway. Keep to the hedge on the left. On the far side go through the metal gate and take the signed footpath on the left through a small wood. When you reach the wooden bridge go across and turn right following the well-trodden path, round close to the riverbank; then go over the small stream across to a wooden gate. Go through the gate, out onto the track and turn left.

After a while you will see a small wooden path marker directing you right into the field (there is no public right of way ahead; the path is well-walked and the route up the field reasonably clear). Make for the corner of the wood in the distance then continue ahead, beside the woods into the field ahead following the track down to meet the lane. Turn left walk down and round, past Fullerton Manor and the mill house, out onto the A3057 and turn right back to the inn (there are no pavements on this stretch of road so take extreme care – it can be very busy). The inn is just over a quarter of a mile away on the right.

The Mill House, Fullerton

The sketch maps in this book are not necessarily to scale but have been drawn to show the maximum amount of detail.

St. Mary The Virgin Silchester, Just showing behind, the Roman town-wall of Calleva Atrebatum, Walk No. 23

The unspoilt Georgian Church at Avington, Walk No. 24

The Tichborne Arms, Tichborne

The Tichborne Arms is an old inn originally dating from the 16th century; the present attractive inn was rebuilt in 1939 after the second of two major fires, and re-thatched in the last few years. It is situated in a lovely rural position, surrounded by fields, close to Tichborne House. There are two bars: The Hampshire, simply furnished with direct access to the delightful beer garden, and the Tichborne, a small comfortable lounge. It is a freehouse with a warm friendly atmosphere well run by the owners, Peter and Chris Byron.

Real ale is still traditionally served straight from casks along the back of the bar. There is a good choice: Directors, Wadsworth's 6X, Courage Best and John Smith's Bitter, plus at least one guest beer.

The inn offers a good choice of bar snacks plus several interesting daily specials, served seven days a week. Everything except the bread is home-made and cooked on the premises. You can choose from a tasty soup, chicken liver pate, filled jacket potatoes, ploughman's, salads, freshly-prepared sandwiches and toasties; one interesting snack is liver and bacon nibbles served with a home-made dip. The changing specials might include pork chops in ginger beer, turkey and leek pie, bacon and onion roll, a chicken curry served with various accompaniments, goulash and lasagne. The home-made puddings spoil you for choice, with lemon cheesecake, syrup sponge, meringues with chocolate, and bread pudding to name but a few.

Children are not allowed inside as there is no family room but dogs are welcome. The inn is open during the week from 11.30 a.m. till 2.30 p.m. and again from 6 p.m. until 11 p.m.

Telephone: (0962) 733760.

The small village of Tichborne is just south of Alresford; it can easily be reached from either the A31 or the A272.

Approx. distance of walk: 4½ miles. O.S. Map No. 185 SU 571/305.

Parking is only possible in the inn's own car park.

A peaceful walk through lovely open countryside. It is fairly flat and easy going, although during wet weather it can be a bit muddy across the fields.

Turn left from the inn and walk up the hill only as far as the track on the right (it is just by the bend in the road). Turn right here and then go immediately left up the signed footpath; it brings you out into the drive in front of the church. Turn left, go down the bridlepath and turn right. After a while it enters a field and further on, in the hedge on the left, are a couple of wooden crossing points. Go over into the adjoining field and bear right, walking towards some farm buildings; go out onto the bridleway, and turn right. After passing a barn the track bears right; on the left are two gates, go through the small one and bear left following the line of the hedge round and up the field to the gate at the top. The path winds its way through a small wood and out through a similar gate on the far side. Continue ahead, down the lane, for about half a mile.

Before reaching Hill Houses, the lane goes off to the right, ignore this but keep straight ahead down a short stony bridleway. At the bottom, just past a cottage, is a signed footpath on the left; turn left here and go up the track, into the field and straight ahead, keeping close to the hedge. When you reach a small wooden gate, turn right into the adjoining field and walk across, keeping close to the hedge. When you reach a small wooden gate, turn right into the adjoining field and walk across, keeping close to the hedge on the right, until you reach the electricity pylon. Go to the right of it and then bear left down the field; go through the gap in the hedge into the lower field, and across to the farm track at the bottom. Turn right, walk through the farm to the road, and straight across down the track opposite. Where the track ends, go into the field on the left and keep straight ahead close to the wire fence until you reach the stile; then turn left and walk straight across the field to the stile beside the gate. Go over a second stile, across the park and out, over the stile on the left beside the gates. Turn right, follow the tarred drive, round to the left and down to the road; turn left back to the inn.

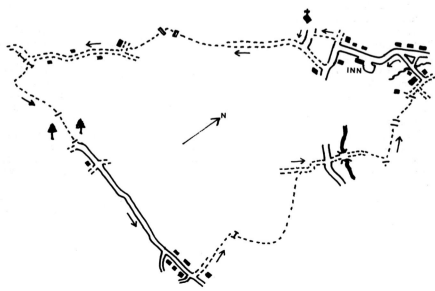

The Bear and Ragged Staff, Timsbury

The Bear and Ragged Staff is a friendly, "wayside inn" occupying a rural position close to the pretty River Test. The interesting inn sign is presumed to be based on the Earl of Warwick's coat of arms, on which the bear and ragged staff is depicted. The inn was refurbished as recently as 1990 and accommodation extended to include a rest area and children's play area. There is a large seating area inside the pub and all the tables, including some very heavy elm ones, are individually named. One wall of the main bar is dominated by a large open fireplace. At the rear of the pub are plenty of picnic-type tables and chairs.

The inn is owned by Whitbread and well run by Peter and Molly Crisp. Three well-conditioned real ales include Strong Country Bitter, Flower's Original and Wethered's S.P.A.

Food is available, you can choose from the set menu or pick one of the daily specials chalked on the blackboard. There are snacks such as homemade soup, pate and "Hampshire mushrooms" served with Stilton cheese and granary bread. There are various grills, fish and chicken dishes. Specials might include "Luma-chiuni Carbonara" – pasta shells, ham, pimentos and herbs in a cheese sauce. "Ratatouille Nicoise au gratin" is aubergines, pimentos, courgettes, garlic and onions stuffed with prawns and mushrooms. Other dishes might include shish kebabs, tandoori chicken, grilled lamb cutlets or a beef and pepper casserole. There is also a separate children's menu.

The inn is open all day, six days a week from 11 a.m. to 11 p.m.; food is only served though between 12 noon and 2 p.m. and between 7 p.m. and 9.30 p.m.

Telephone: (0794) 68602.

The inn is on the A3057 Romsey to Stockbridge road, about 1¼ miles north of Timsbury.

Approx. distance of walk: 4¼ miles. O.S. Map No. 185 SU 335/258.

The inn has two car parks: a small area at the front and a much larger park at the rear.

A beautiful scenic walk through through the lovely Test Valley – one of my favourites. The walk is hilly in places, fairly dry underfoot and easy to follow. It takes you across fields, through woods, back and forth over the River Test, down country lanes, along the Test Way and through the grounds of Mottisfont Abbey and historic Mottisfont village.

Start from the front of the inn and go up the lane towards Michelmarsh. Near the top, when you meet another lane, turn left and walk down until you reach the road junction. Ahead of you is a gravel track with two small wooden gates (the footpath is signed); go up the drive, past the cottage and into the field (again it is signed). Follow the path straight across the centre of the field and up to meet a gravel track at the top. Turn left, past the farm buildings, following the track round and into the field on the right. Turn right and make your way across to the left-hand corner of the far hedge (you will find the yellow path marker on the corner post). Continue ahead walking to the left away from the corner to a gap in the far hedge (it is well marked). The path goes steeply down through a thicket to a stile at the bottom. Go over, across to a second stile, into the field and bear right down to the stile beside the metal gate.

Walk straight across the road and through the fencing, down to the tarred drive and straight ahead, over the bridge and through the gate into the field (the footpath is well signed, follow the white posts). On the far side is a stile which brings you out on to a gravel drive; turn left past the cottage and continue round, over the bridge, past some buildings until you come to a stile set in the hedge on the left. Go into the field and bear left across to a group of large oaks (you will see the path-marker on the farthest oak). Continue walking across in the same direction, only as far as a path-marker post in front of a large tree. At this point turn right and walk up to the top of the field, out into the road and turn left (You get a good view of Mottisfont Abbey – an Augustinian priory built in the 12th-century. It is now owned by The National Trust and open to the public from April to end of September on Wednesdays only from 2 p.m. until 6 p.m.

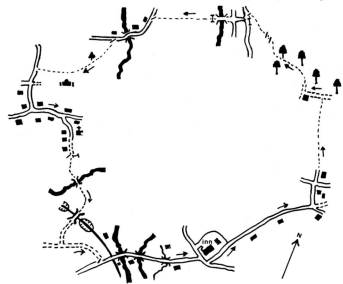

85

The grounds are open daily, except Sunday and Monday, from 2.30 p.m. till 6 p.m.).

Walk down to the village centre – if you are there at the right time they serve refreshments on the village green. Continue down, past the post office and take the turning on the right to the church (it is very old dating from 676 A.D.). The road eventually merges with a grass track leading down to a field. Go over the stile and straight across to meet the river Dun. On the left is a bridge; cross the river and go up the path into the woods. It passes over the railway bridge before widening to meet a track; turn left and walk down the track to the road, go over the stile and turn left, over the level crossing, down the lane to the inn.

The beautiful river Test photographed from two different points during the walk

'Pannage' Pasturage of swine – pigs set free in the New Forest to forage for acorns.

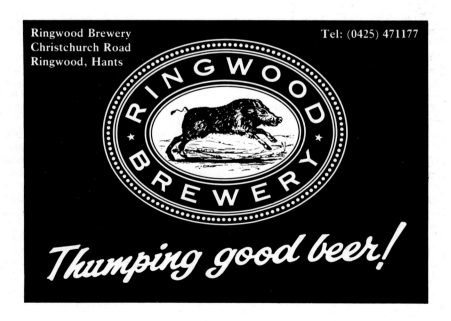

The Brushmakers Arms, Upham

The Brushmakers Arms is an interesting old inn: the building goes back 600 years and has alternated between being a pub and a brushmaker's workshop. I am reliably informed that Cromwell once stayed here while his men were garrisoned up the road. The inn is also reputed to have its own resident ghost. Today it is a quaint, comfortable well-decorated pub with one main bar and an adjoining seating area, both heated by the same real fire in winter, all around the walls are a collection of different brushes. At the back is a lovely lawn and terraced beer garden with picnic benches and tubs of flowers. The inn is a freehouse well run by the resident owners, Ann and Kevin Dickinson.

Two real ales are on offer: draught Bass and Morland Old Masters.

A good food menu is available but served lunchtimes only, between 12 noon and 2 p.m. There are various snacks such as sandwiches, ploughman's and home-made soup like bacon and lentil; other dishes include macaroni cheese, a home-made curry and grilled gammon plus a seafood platter. There is a blackboard in the bar listing the daily specials, which may include stuffed ham, spinach and prawns with cheese sauce, chicken merango, steak and kidney pie, lasagne or cauliflower cheese with garlic bread. A choice of sweets can include plum crumble and apple and blackberry pie.

Children are welcome and dogs allowed in the bar areas but not in the garden.

Opening times during the week are from 11 a.m. till 2.30 p.m. and from 7 p.m. till 11 p.m. Sunday hours are in keeping with all other pubs.

Telephone: (048 96) 231.

The village lies east of Eastleigh and a couple of miles north of Bishops Waltham. It is best reached from the B2177 by taking the turning at Lower Upham. From the M27 go to Botley then Bishop's Waltham on the B3035.

Approx. distance of walk: 3 miles. O.S. Map No. 185 SU 540/206.

Parking is limited to the lane outside the inn or the lane by the duck pond.

Upham is a pretty, isolated village surrounded by peaceful rolling countryside. The walk is fairly short and easy going down quiet country lanes and along wide, established tracks. It is ideal for the whole family and suitable for all weather conditions.

Leave the inn and turn right, then left at the road junction. Walk past the duck pond and take the turning on the left (signed to Corhampton). Follow the lane for some distance, down the hill, past the farm, and up until you eventually reach a narrow lane on the left before reaching the road junction. Turn left down this lane (it is fairly long and peaceful). Walk past a house until you reach a track on the left opposite a red-bricked house (there is a right-of-way sign). Turn left and walk up the track. After only a short distance take the track on the right – you will see the wooden footpath sign. The track rises steeply between fields then levels out, emerging into a playing field. Keep to the right and go to the far side of the field, out into the road and turn left, down the lane back to the inn.

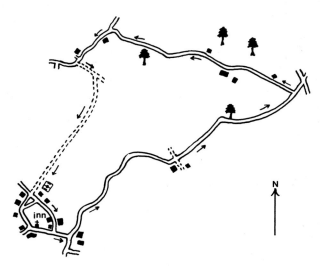

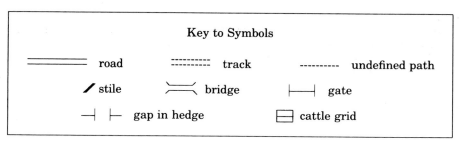

Key to Symbols

road   track   undefined path

stile   bridge   gate

gap in hedge   cattle grid

The George Inn, Vernham Dean

High up in northern Hampshire, close to the Wiltshire and Berkshire borders is the isolated village of Vernham Dean. The pretty George Inn, a friendly village local, built in the 16th-century has timbered brick and flint walls supporting an attractive tiled roof which curves around the upper storey windows. Inside there are three inter-connected bars each with its own fireplace and large log fires in winter; and all have heavily timbered walls and beamed ceiling and the main bar a large inglenook fireplace with its own seating. The furnishings are simple, comfortable and in keeping with the rest of the inn. Outside there are a couple of picnic benches and a lawned beer garden at the back. The inn is owned by Marstons and well run by the tenants, Mary and Philip Perry who took over during 1989.

Two well-kept real ales are served by hand pump, Marston's Pedigree and Burton Best.

Good bar food is available both at lunchtime and in the evening. The menu, changed daily, is chalked on the blackboard in the bar; everything is made and cooked on the premises. For just a snack you can have one of their tasty ploughman's of home-cooked ham or mature cheddar, pate, various toasties, quiche or a selection of salads. Hot meals vary from lasagne, liver and bacon, cottage pie, or cheese, bacon and onion pie to one of the specialities such as 'George Inn mushrooms' – garlic-flavoured mushrooms topped with cheese and bacon.

Opening times during the week can vary from 11 a.m. until 2.30 p.m. and from 6 p.m. till 11 p.m. Overnight accommodation is available.

Telephone: (0264) 87279.

The inn is best reached from the A343, Andover to Newbury road. Take the turning for Upton at Hurstbourne Tarrant; the next village is Vernham Dean. The George is on the right after the school.

Approx. distance of walk: 3½ miles. O.S. Map No. 174 SU 342/566.

The inn has its own car park at the front, but it is safe to park in the lane outside.

Vernham Dean is a lovely peaceful village in the most north westerly tip of Hampshire. The walk is easy, mostly on farmland and country lanes, but at one point it does climb steeply up through a meadow.

Leave the inn and turn right. Walk past the telephone box and turn up the gravel track on the left, just past Underwood cottage. Go over the stile beside the gate, up and over another stile into the field. Keeping to the track beside the hedge, walk up and round, turning left about half-way up onto a signed track. At first the track passes through a wooded area before dipping down into a valley; at this point do not continue ahead up into the woods but turn right along the valley until you reach a stile in the metal fence ahead of you. Go over into the meadow and turn left, keeping close to the woods, follow the path up to the top (it is well signed, look for the small wooden posts). Go through the gap into the field, bear right, and walk straight across to an opening in the far hedge, out into the lane and turn left.

The lane is fairly long, but quite peaceful with very little traffic; eventually when you meet the road at the bottom go across, over the stile in the wire fence, and bear left across the field to a stile beside a gate in the hedge opposite. Go up the field, keeping close to the wire fence on your right, bear left at the top and take the path off to the right into a small wooded copse. The path passes behind a house, goes through the churchyard and out through a gate into the lane. Turn left back to the inn (a distance of about ¾ of a mile).

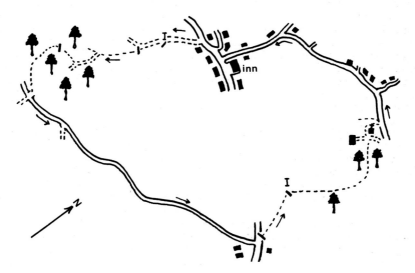

The sketch maps in this book are not necessarily to scale but have been drawn to show the maximum amount of detail.

The Boot, Littledown, Vernham Street

This quaint, thatched, brick-and-flint inn, built in the 15th century, has changed a little over the years. Located in a lovely tranquil spot; it was originally a cobblers (the origin of the name), which managed to survive destruction following the black plague that ravaged the near-by village of Vernham Street. Inside there are two small inter-connected bars, both low-beamed with white-panelled walls; one has a dartboard – the other, simply-furnished, has a large open fireplace with a warm log fire in winter. Across the entrance porch is a small room for private or family use. A large double-glazed, heated conservatory has recently been added to extend the dining area. Outside a large area is lawned with tables, chairs and picnic benches. The Boot is a free-house well-run by the owners, Neale and Helen Baker.

In the best traditions of good innkeeping, real ale is still served straight from the cask. You can normally choose from Badger Best, Wadsworth's 6X, Marston's Pedigree and Burton Bitter.

Bar snacks are served up to 2.30 p.m. lunchtimes and 9.30 p.m. in the evening. You can choose from the set menu or pick one of the daily specials chalked on the blackboard. Apart from sandwiches and ploughman's, various salads offer a choice of meat, fish or vegetarian; a popular snack is their half pint of prawns with a dip. Several basket meals include wings of fire and a fisherman's platter. Depending on the time of year the daily specials can include home-made soup or mackerel pate, home-made steak and kidney pie or an Indian platter. Children are well-catered for.

A good choice of sweets include locally made ice-cream and spotted dick. Various wines are available by the glass or bottle.

The inn is open during the week from 12 noon till 3 p.m. and again from 6 p.m. (7 p.m. in the winter). The inn is closed on Mondays, except for bank holidays. Telephone: (026 487) 213.

The inn is best reached from the A343, Andover to Newbury road. At Hurstbourne Tarrant take the road on the left to Vernham Dean, turning right in the village to Vernham Street; keep going until you reach the inn.

Approx. distance of walk: 3¼ miles. O.S. Map No. 174 SU 352/581.

There is plenty of parking space beside the inn.

A most enjoyable walk in this northerly tip of west Hampshire – it could easily be called the three counties walk as it actually passes through Wiltshire and Berkshire as well as Hampshire. It is easy going, reasonably dry, and ideal for the whole family. Part of the walk is on the Test Way, the rest through woods and along country lanes.

Leave the inn and turn right at the crossroads, up the lane in the direction of Buttermere. Just before the lane bears round to the left you will see a gravel track on the right (there is a 'right of way' sign). Turn right and walk up to the top and go into the field on the left (it is signed). This point, although not marked, is where the three counties meet.

Keeping close to the hedge on the right, walk across to the far side, following the grassy track into the woods; the path emerges beside a field and leads down to meet the Test Way. Turn right and follow the track, for some distance, into and through the lovely Coombe Wood. Continue past a small red building until you reach a track on the right; turn right here and go up as far as a small flint and brick building. Opposite, on the right, is a signed footpath; go up this path (it rises steeply through woods to a stile at the top). Go over into the field and straight across along the track on the far side, out into the lane and turn right, back to the inn.

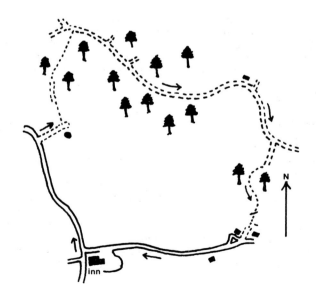

The Cartwheel Inn, Whitsbury

The Cartwheel must surely be everyone's idea of the ideal country pub. Situated in the tranquil village of Whitsbury, in an area of outstanding natural beauty, it was originally two cottages built in 1796. Around 1860 it became an inn and was just known as the Wheel. At that time it was supplied with beer from Carter's brewery in Ringwood. It has changed hands several times since and is now a freehouse very well run by its friendly owners, Jeanie and Ian. There is one main cosy bar with an open fireplace, a separate games room and a cosy candlelit dining room seating up to twenty. Outside there is a lovely beer garden with a summer barbecue area and a special children's play area with rockers, climbing frame and a tunnel slide.

The bar is extremely well-stocked with a large range of drinks; six hand pumps serve well-conditioned real ale chosen from 36 different brews: delights such as Hook Norton's Best, Marsden's 6X and occasionally Fuller's 'Mr Harry' (I am told that it is only brewed three times a year).

There is an extensive bar menu catering for all tastes, including children and vegetarians. The inn is popular for its snack meals, especially its large range of sandwiches and tasty filled jacket potatoes; there are 13 fillings including the 'Cartwheel' special, ham, tomato, mushroom, onion and cheese. From a selection of starters you can choose home-made soup, smoked trout and seafood-au-gratin – cod and crabmeat in a creamy sauce topped with prawns and grilled cheese. Tasty home-cooked dishes include steak and kidney pudding, chilli and lasagne. There are various steaks and fish dishes plus a few daily specials listed on the black-boards around the bar, such as fresh crab salad and wholemeal pizza. Four vegetarian dishes include cashew paella, pizza and the inn's own 'parmagiana' – pieces of pasta, diced peppers and mushrooms in a cream sauce with a cheese topping. A good range of sweets include several sundaes made from New Forest real dairy ice-cream, produced from local Jersey herds.

The inn is open during the week from 11 a.m. till 2.30 p.m. and 6 p.m. till 11 p.m. Telephone: (07253) 362.

Whitsbury is best reached from Fordingbridge off the B3078. The inn is in the main street in the centre of the village.

Approx. distance of walk: 5 miles. O.S. Map No. 184 SU 128/188.

Park in the inn's own car park or in the road outside.

Whitsbury is a lovely tranquil village, beautifully kept, and surrounded by delightful scenery. It is famous for its racing stables and stud which is home to 'Rhyme and Reason', the winner of the 1988 Grand National. The walk is quite long but easy going, for the most part on wide tracks. It passes through woodland, beside paddocks and takes you through the historic grounds of Breamore House (with its ancient miz-maze).

From the inn turn right, walking up through the village until you reach the stables at the top. Ahead of you is a signed bridleway; take this bridleway between two white fenced paddocks, round to the right and then left to the bottom of the hill. Go across the track and over the stile in the hedge opposite, walking up the field through the gate at the top and out onto a grassy track. Continue ahead, entering the wood beside the Dutch barn, out through the gate on the far side, across the field and over the stile on to the grassy track.

Turn right and, keeping close to the hedge on the left, continue walking until you meet a gravel track (You can take a detour up to

the small wood on the right if you want to see the ancient 'miz-maze'). The track takes you through Breamore Wood, carpeted with bluebells in spring and a pink mantle of red campion and foxgloves in summertime.

As you emerge from the woods you pass historic Braemore House (it is open to the public Tuesdays, Wednesdays, Thursdays, Saturdays, Sundays and bank holidays from 2 p.m. till 5.30 p.m.). As you leave the House through the main gates, turn right and follow the gravel track round behind the tea rooms and the countryside museum – well worth a visit – past chocolate box cottages and out into the lane. Continue ahead through the village of Upper Street and take

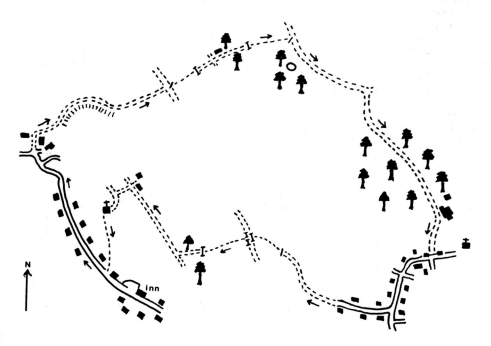

N

inn

the turning on the right by the letter-box. Just beyond a thatched cottage the lane merges into a track; keep going straight ahead until you reach a stile leading into a field (the footpath is signed).

At the far side go out through the metal gate, across the track, through the two metal gates opposite and, keeping close to the hedge on the right, walk up the field to the far side. Go through the metal gate and take the track ahead of you into the woods. When you meet another track turn right and follow it between woodland and paddocks until you reach a bungalow on the right. Take the track on the left between two fields and then bear left round to the church. Go through the gate, round to the front of the churchyard and out through the small gate. Follow the path down, turning left when you reach the village.

Breamore House